Life Insurance: A Consumer's Handbook

LIFEINSURANCELIFEINSURANCELIFEINSURANCE

Life Insurance
A Consumer's Handbook

Second Edition

Joseph M. Belth

Indiana University Press

Bloomington

LIFEINSURANCELIFEINSURANCELIFEINSURANCE

Manufactured in the United States of America

Library of Congress Cataloging in Publication Data

Belth, Joseph M.
  Life insurance.

  Includes index.
  1. Insurance, Life—United States—Handbooks, manuals,
etc. I. Title.
HG8951.B45   1985   368.3'2'0029   84-47705
ISBN 0-253-14840-5
ISBN 0-253-20346-5 (pbk.)

4 5 6 7 8 93 92 91 90

To the memory of
Irving and Helen Rose Bright Belth

Contents

Tables

LIFEINSURANCELIFEINSURANCELIFEINSURANCE

Figures

Preface

On May 3, 1984, a hearing was held before the Subcommittee on Monopolies and Commercial Law of the Committee on the Judiciary of the United States House of Representatives. I testified that consumers do not receive adequate information about life insurance, and I made these comments about the future:

> Developments during the past twenty years suggest that rigorous disclosure requirements will never be mandated by the state insurance departments. Industry opposition to such requirements is too strong. Nor do recent developments at the federal level offer any hope for consumers.

Congressman Peter W. Rodino, Jr. (D-NJ), who conducted the hearing as subcommittee chairman, stated succinctly: "You're a pessimist." I replied succinctly: "A realist, Mr. Chairman."

Life insurance consumers need certain important information to make sound decisions in their own interests. The content of this book was influenced by my belief that consumers must take the initiative and obtain the information for themselves.

The first edition, which was published in 1973, was written to fill a gap. The only books available to life insurance consumers were written either by critics of the industry or by defenders of the industry. The critics' books displayed a lack of knowledge about the fundamentals of life insurance, and the defenders' books did not provide specific guidance for consumers.

This second edition is similar to the first in some respects. For example, it covers three areas you must consider: how much life insurance you need, what kind of life insurance you should buy, and from what company you should buy it. It also explains how to select a life insurance agent.

However, the second edition differs from the first in important ways. First, it is designed to help consumers obtain for themselves the information they need for making sound decisions. Consistent with that objective, it contains instructions on how to assemble the necessary data, how to perform price calculations, and how to evaluate the results.

Second, direct price comparisons among the offerings of different companies are avoided and discouraged. These comparisons are fraught with danger because of some technical elements of noncomparability that have cropped up in recent years. Instead, the book contains instructions on how to identify low-priced policies, and suggests some companies for buyers to consider.

Third, a chapter has been added to assist the owners of existing life insurance policies in determining whether serious consideration should be given to replacing their policies. This material was considered important because of widespread replacement activity, some of which is justified and some of which is detrimental to policyowners.

Comments and suggestions from readers would be welcomed. Please write directly to the author at P. O. Box 245, Ellettsville, IN 47429.

I am grateful to the many persons who assisted, directly or indirectly, in the preparation of this book. Professor John D. Long, my longtime colleague at Indiana University, is a constant source of encouragement. Several graduate students and numerous undergraduate students furnished a testing ground for the ideas presented. The staff of the Indiana University Press handled the publication details.

Five individuals read and commented upon a preliminary draft of this book: two academicians, William T. Beadles and Robert I. Mehr; two actuaries, E. J. Moorhead and Larry N. Stern; and a writer, John R. Dorfman. I am indebted to these readers, especially Professor Mehr for his extraordinarily helpful comments and suggestions.

I owe a considerable debt to Indiana University's School of Business. It has contributed significantly to this and other projects by preserving an atmosphere conducive to the teaching, research, and public service efforts of the faculty.

I owe the greatest debt of all to my wife, Marjorie. She cheerfully handles more than her share of the responsibilities in our house. By so doing, she contributes immeasurably to my writing efforts.

All of these persons and organizations must be absolved from responsibility for the statements of fact and expressions of opinion set forth in this book. The author alone assumes full responsibility for the views expressed and for any errors that may remain.

Life Insurance: A Consumer's Handbook

Chapter 1

Introduction

The purpose of this book is to help you buy and manage your life insurance efficiently.

- How much life insurance should you buy?
- What type of life insurance should you buy?
- What company should you buy from?
- What agent should you buy from?
- Should you replace any of your existing life insurance?

This book is designed to answer these five big questions. It also discusses suppliers of life insurance other than commercial life insurance companies, the "fine print" in the policy contract, issues to keep in mind when you buy life insurance, how to manage your existing life insurance, and a variety of other relevant topics.

The Mythology of Life Insurance

This book is needed because consumers often do not receive accurate and useful information about life insurance. Instead, many are exposed primarily to two sets of mythology—one offered by or on behalf of the life insurance business, and the other by various critics of the business. Among the myths emanating from at least some segments of the business are the following:

- "All life insurance companies charge about the same price." (The fact is that there are large price differences among companies for essentially the same type of life insurance coverage.)

- "Life insurance companies are regulated adequately by the states, so it doesn't matter what company you patronize." (Actually, regulation is much weaker in some states than in others, and some of the requirements constitute inadequate protection for consumers.)

- "Life insurance companies, particularly the mutual companies, are operated for the benefit of policyowners and their families." (Actually, the life insurance companies, including the mutual companies, are in business to make a profit, just as other businesses are.)

Among the myths promulgated by the critics of the life insurance business are the following:

- "The life insurance companies are overcharging the public through the use of outdated mortality tables that overstate death rates." (The facts are that up-to-date mortality tables are used in many of the companies' calculations, and, moreover, the choice of a mortality table, in and of itself, may have little to do with how well the policyowner fares financially in his or her dealings with a life insurance company.)

- "The type of life insurance that includes a savings component is more expensive than pure life insurance protection." (The truth is that if life insurance is carefully purchased—following the procedures described in this book—the price of the protection in the type of life insurance that includes a savings component can compare favorably to the price of pure life insurance protection.)

- "Life insurance agents are scoundrels who are exploiting the public." (Actually, some agents are conscientious and helpful. Also, some of what inferior agents say and do is learned from their companies, and such agents may not realize that some of what they are taught is slanted, misleading, or false.)

How to Use This Book

The book should be read from cover to cover. To assure that less thorough readers will also benefit, it has been organized like a reference book, so that the desired topics can be selected.

The book necessarily contains some technical words and phrases. These terms are explained when they first appear. They are also included in the index, which can be used to locate discussions of them as they occur throughout the book. Numerous cross references are used in the text, and an outline of each chapter is included in the table of contents.

Summary of the Book

Chapter 2 deals with the first of the five big questions with which this book is concerned: How much life insurance should you buy? Emphasis is placed on the personal nature of such a determination. The first step is an estimation of the financial requirements of your family in the event of your death. The second step is an estimation of the financial resources available to your family in the event of your death. The amount of life insurance you should buy, then, is the difference between the financial requirements and the financial resources.

Chapters 3 through 6 deal with the second of the five big questions: What type of life insurance should you buy? This question should be approached only after you have determined how much life insurance you need. Chapter 3 describes two major types of life insurance that can meet the needs of nearly all buyers, two relatively new types of life insurance that may be attractive, and three important riders that may be attached to many of the basic policy forms. Chapter 4 describes various other types of available life insurance. Chapter 5 describes the nature of the savings component in those types of life insurance that include savings; the purpose of the chapter is to help you decide whether and to what extent you should combine savings with life insurance. Chapter 6 explains how you should make your choice between the two major types of life insurance described in Chapter 3.

Chapter 7 deals with the third of the five big questions: What company should you buy from? This question should be considered only after you have determined how much life insurance you need and what type of policy or policies to buy. The first section of the chapter explains the company identification problem, which arises because so many companies have sound-alike names. The second section contains suggestions on how to be assured that the company with which you deal is financially strong. The third section contains two listings of suggested companies—one for each of the two major types of life insurance.

Chapter 8 contains a discussion of the price of life insurance. This chapter is important because the subject is one about which there is great misunderstanding.

Chapters 9 through 11 deal with life insurance contract provisions. Chapter 9 discusses provisions that are included in life insurance contracts generally. Chapter 10 discusses provisions that are restricted to one-year renewable term policies. Chapter 11 discusses provisions that are limited to cash-value policies. Although these chapters contain considerable detail, emphasis is placed on the important points that you should understand in order to protect yourself and your beneficiary against potential future problems.

Chapter 12 deals with the fourth of the five big questions: What agent should you buy from? The chapter also discusses why most commercial life insurance companies use agents and what agents are supposed to do. This chapter is important because most of the life insurance in the United States is sold through agents, and you probably will deal with one.

Chapters 13 through 15 include discussions of a number of miscellaneous subjects. Chapter 13 describes some of the sources through which life insurance is available without agents. Chapter 14 covers several points that are relevant at the time a person applies for life insurance. Chapter 15 contains a number of suggestions to be followed after a person buys life insurance.

Chapter 16 deals with the fifth of the five big questions: Should you replace any of your existing life insurance? The chapter describes a procedure for evaluating an existing life insurance policy. If you follow the procedure carefully, you can determine whether you should consider the replacement of one or more of your policies.

Chapter 17 is the author's conclusion. The chapter describes the ignorance, complexity, and apathy that permeate the life insurance market, and explains how the combined effect of these three characteristics produces fertile ground for the exploitation of consumers. The chapter also describes what is and is not being done to improve the life insurance market for the benefit of life insurance consumers.

Appendix A explains some of the arithmetic needed in estimating your financial requirements and your financial resources. Appendix B lists those life insurance companies that have received top ratings for ten consecutive years from a major publisher that analyzes the financial strength of insurance companies. Appendix C shows the addresses of the various state insurance departments. Appendix D explains the formula for calculating yearly prices. Appendix E explains the formula for calculating yearly rates of return.

The Importance of Life Insurance

Do not underestimate the importance of life insurance in your financial affairs. Thousands upon thousands of dollars may be lost to you or to your family if you fail to arrange your life insurance properly. Indeed, the very survival of your family may depend upon the care with which you make the critical decisions about your life insurance.

Chapter 2

How to Measure Your Life Insurance Needs

The determination of your life insurance needs is an individual matter. No hard-and-fast rules apply to everyone, because no two people view their circumstances in the same way.

You might ask, "How much life insurance is owned by the typical person in my age and income bracket?" Even if data were available to answer this question, the information wouldn't mean much. Many individuals own little or no life insurance, many others own substantial amounts that are far short of their needs, and some own substantial amounts that bear a reasonable relationship to their needs. The typical breadwinner probably is underinsured by a significant amount. For example, many families with less than $50,000 of life insurance probably need more than $200,000, if their life insurance needs were estimated realistically.

A life insurance agent may suggest that you should own life insurance equal to at least five times (or perhaps seven or even ten times) your annual earnings. Or an agent may suggest that your life insurance premiums should be about 5 percent (or perhaps 7 or even 10 percent) of your annual earnings. Such rules of thumb are meaningless.

Consider, for example, two hypothetical families that have the same family status, income, assets, and liabilities. The two families differ in only one respect. One believes that in the event of the breadwinner's death a substantial income will be needed for one year, followed by a reduced income for another four years. The other family believes that in the event of the breadwinner's death a substantial income will be needed for thirty years. For the first family, the financial requirements, including life insurance, may be equal to about one year's earnings. For the second family, the financial requirements, including life insurance, may be equal to more than ten years' earnings.

Here are some of the difficult, personal questions you and your spouse must ask yourselves:

- Will your spouse be able and willing to work in gainful employment following your death, and, if so, how much will your spouse be able to earn?
- Will your spouse remarry?
- Will your spouse be able and willing to move in with relatives?
- Will your spouse be willing to dispose of your present house in order to move into a less expensive one?

You may want to answer all such questions in the negative. Or you may want to answer one or more in the positive. Or you may want to work out your life insurance needs under various assumptions and make your decision after comparing the results. The method described in this chapter is flexible enough to permit any of these approaches.

The procedure described in this chapter is based upon the assumption that your death occurs immediately. The financial requirements of your family and the financial resources that would be available to them are discussed. Life insurance is a means for filling any gap between these requirements and your available resources. Once you master the procedure, you can repeat the steps every two or three years (assuming you continue to live), to check the continuing adequacy of your life insurance.

Financial Requirements

Your family will have financial requirements to meet after your death. They may be grouped for convenience into three categories: final expenses, debts, and income needs.

Final Expenses

Funeral expenses will be incurred. (Even in the absence of a funeral, the expenses of disposing of your body will be incurred.) The expenses of settling your estate will be incurred. Federal and state death taxes, as well as local property taxes that are commonly lagged by one year, will be incurred. These expenses will have to be paid either immediately or within a short time after your death.

These final expenses may be about 10 percent of your estate, provided you are a person of modest means. For example, if the total of the property you own—including bank accounts, stocks, bonds, real estate, and life insurance—amounts to between $100,000 and $200,000, the final expenses probably will be in the range of $10,000 to $20,000. For a family with a much larger amount of property, the final expenses probably will be more than 10 percent of the estate. You may want to ask your family's attorney for an estimate of your final expenses.

Debts

Your family may have to pay off various short-term obligations, including charge accounts, installment loans, and short-term notes. The unpaid balances of these items should be added and the total considered among the financial requirements of the family immediately after your death.

Long-term obligations, such as the mortgage on your house, may be viewed in one of two ways. You may want to treat the mortgage in the same manner as other debts and consider the unpaid balance (including any prepayment penalties) as an immediate financial requirement of your family upon your death. Or you may want to view the mortgage loan payments as a continuing cost of housing your family and consider that cost in establishing the family's income needs.

Income Needs

In terms of its impact on the final result, the most important of your financial requirements is the income your family will need following your death. Presumably the figures you select here will be based in part on your current earnings and on various other considerations to be discussed in the following paragraphs.

To determine the income requirements of your family, you must consider several things. First, thought should be given to the question of whether your spouse may become or will continue to be gainfully employed. If so, your family's income requirements will be smaller than if you assume your spouse will not be gainfully employed.

Second, the remarriage question should be examined. If the assumption is that your spouse will remarry, your family's income requirements will be for a shorter period of time than if the contrary assumption is made.

Third, the way you handle your mortgage loan should be consistent. If you decide to treat it as a debt to be paid at your death, the income requirements of your family will be smaller than if you decide to treat future mortgage payments as part of the cost of housing your family.

Fourth, an interest rate must be selected for use in calculating the amount needed to provide the required income. Suppose your family needs $18,000 per year for ten years after your death. The total is $180,000. However, because interest can be earned, an amount less than $180,000 is needed to produce an income of $18,000 per year for ten years. For example, if the funds are assumed to earn 6 percent interest, the amount needed at death to provide $18,000 per year for ten years is about $140,000. How this figure is computed is explained in Appendix A.

The choice of the interest rate is important. It has a powerful effect on the results, particularly when the income requirements stretch over a long period of time. A conservative interest rate should be chosen—one that your spouse can safely expect to earn after income taxes. Many savings accounts today earn 5½ percent, and higher rates are readily available through certificates of deposit and other forms of savings. An interest rate of 6 percent is used in most of the illustrations in this book.

Fifth, you should consider the effect of inflation. If your family receives $18,000 per year for ten years, and if inflation continues, their income will decline in real terms. To offset inflation, an income that increases in dollar terms should be provided. You can approximate the effect of expected inflation by using in your calculations an interest rate that is reduced by an assumed inflation rate. For example, if you use a 6 percent interest assumption, but also want to assume an inflation rate of 4 percent, you can approximate the effect of inflation on your financial requirements by using 2 percent interest (6 percent minus 4 percent) in your calculations. Appendix A shows that it will take about $165,000 to provide $18,000 per year for ten years at 2 percent interest. This figure is about $25,000 larger than the earlier figure of $140,000 calculated at 6 percent. This $25,000 difference is the approximate impact of a 4 percent inflation rate assumption on your financial requirements.*

When you have decided how much income your family will need and how long they will need it, and when you have decided on the interest rate to be used in the calculations, the next step is to find out how much will be needed now (assuming you die now) to provide the required income. Appendix A shows how to make the calculations.

The example given earlier involved an assumption that the family's income needs will be constant. In some cases, however, the income requirements will be non-uniform, as in the case of children's college expenses. Appendix A explains how to make the calculations when the income requirements are not uniform.

Total Requirements

After you have estimated your final expenses, debts, and income needs, add these figures to arrive at the total financial requirements in the event of your immediate death. The next step is to estimate the financial resources available to meet these requirements.

---

*You should assume a conservative combination of interest and inflation rates. If you assume a high interest rate because you have little confidence in the ability of the federal government to keep interest rates under control, you should also assume a high inflation rate.

Financial Resources

Your family will have some resources to meet their financial requirements after your death. These resources may be grouped into three
categories: life insurance, Social Security, and other assets.

Life Insurance

Determine the total death benefits provided by your present life
insurance policies. Don't forget to include the death benefits under
any government life insurance you may have, any group life insurance you may have through your employer or union, and any
group life insurance you may have as a member of an association.

Some of your policies may provide for additional death benefits in
the event of accidental death. Frequently such benefits are called
"double indemnity." You may also have some policies that provide
death benefits only in the event of certain forms of accidental death.
An example is an automobile club policy providing coverage only in
the event of death in an automobile accident. Although much publicity often accompanies accidental death, most deaths are caused by
illnesses. Thus, to be on the conservative side in listing your resources,
you should disregard death benefits that are payable only if death is
the result of an accident.

Social Security

Nearly everyone is covered by Social Security, a program that provides retirement benefits, disability benefits, Medicare benefits, and
survivors' benefits. The survivors' benefits are monthly income payments, and they can be substantial, particularly for families with
young children.

Suppose you were born in 1950 and have worked continuously in
jobs covered by Social Security since you were 22. Also, suppose your
earnings have always exceeded the maximum on which Social Security taxes have been paid. (The maximum earnings since 1972 are
shown in Table 1.)

Suppose your wife was born in 1952, and you have two small children. If you die in 1985, Social Security will provide a monthly income to your family. This income will be a combination of a mother's
benefit and a benefit for each child. The mother's benefit is payable as
long as she has your children under age 16 in her care; this benefit

Table 1
*Maximum Earnings Subject
to Social Security Taxes*

Year	Maximum Earnings
1972	$ 9,000
1973	10,800
1974	13,200
1975	14,100
1976	15,300
1977	16,500
1978	17,700
1979	22,900
1980	25,900
1981	29,700
1982	32,400
1983	35,700
1984	37,800
1985	39,600

ceases if she dies or remarries, and is reduced, possibly to zero, depending on the amount of her annual earnings. Each child's benefit is payable until the child reaches 18, or, if the child remains in high school, until the child reaches 19.

In your case, the total survivors' benefits payable to your family will be about $16,000 per year until the first child becomes ineligible, and then about $10,000 per year until the second child becomes ineligible. If the mother's benefit terminates because she dies, remarries, or earns a substantial income, the children's benefits will be about $10,000 per year until the first child becomes ineligible, and then about $5,000 per year until the second child becomes ineligible.

Appendix A will help you calculate the value of your Social Security survivors' benefits. To be consistent with the calculation of the value of your family's income requirements, use the same interest and inflation rates here. You are then assuming that the benefit structure of Social Security will keep up with inflation; this assumption is not unreasonable in view of the cost-of-living adjustments built into the Social Security benefit formula.

When you calculate the value of your Social Security survivors' benefits, consider only the benefits payable over the period for which the income is required. For example, if you included ten years of income in the calculation of your family's financial requirements, you should include Social Security survivors' benefits only for ten years, even though the benefits might be payable for a longer period.

Social Security also provides a monthly income for a widow who is aged 60 or over. In your case, for example, given the situation described above, your widow's income will be about $6,000 per year beginning at her age 60.

This discussion of Social Security is brief and incomplete. Also, the figures apply only to the illustrated case. Social Security survivors' benefits have substantial value and therefore are an important part of the resources available to your family. For these reasons, you should obtain an estimate of the survivors' benefits payable to your family if you die now. Several steps should be followed to obtain such an estimate.

First, list your earnings that have been subject to Social Security taxes for each year beginning with the year in which you became aged 22. If you were born before 1929, list the figures only for the years beginning with 1951.

Second, obtain from your local Social Security office a postcard to be mailed to the Baltimore data center for a statement of your Social Security account. This statement is not a substitute for the first step above, but will help you verify the earnings figures you have listed. The statement will also help you determine whether any errors have occurred in the crediting of earnings to your account.

Third, contact your local Social Security office for assistance in obtaining an estimate of the survivors' benefits payable to your family if you die now. To estimate your survivors' benefits, the first step is to estimate your basic retirement benefit. If you want to see how such an estimate is made, obtain from your local Social Security office a booklet entitled "Estimating Your Social Security Retirement Check."

You must keep up with changes in Social Security benefit levels, because these changes occur frequently. Follow the above procedure to obtain an estimate of survivors' benefits each time you review your life insurance program.

Other Assets

Add the current values of the other assets that will be available to your family at your death. Included here should be checking accounts, savings accounts, savings and loan accounts, credit union accounts, savings bonds, mutual funds, marketable securities, marketable real estate other than your house, the death benefit under any pension plan in which you are a participant, and the accumulation (minus income taxes that will have to be paid) in such programs as individual retirement accounts, tax-sheltered annuities, and Keogh accounts. To be on the conservative side, you may want to include securities and real estate at less than current market values.

Many other items may be included here, depending upon how you view them. You may want to include the current market value of your house, but you should be consistent with the approach you took earlier in estimating your family's income requirements. If you figured the income requirements at a low level because you already own your house, do not include it as an asset here. But if you included in your income requirements a substantial amount for the cost of housing, it is appropriate to include in your assets the current market value of your house.

The same observation applies to your automobiles. If your family's income requirements included a substantial amount for transportation, you may want to include in your assets the depreciated value of your automobiles.

You may want to include here such items as stamp collections, coin collections, valuable antiques, art objects, horses, and so on. The basic test for inclusion should be the liquidity of the item in question.

If you or your spouse may inherit property, you will have to judge whether the potential inheritance should be included among the resources available to your family in the event of your death. If so, you will have to determine the value that should be placed on it in the planning process.

If you have a substantial interest in a business in which you are a principal, and if you believe the business will help your family meet its financial requirements after your death, you may want to include its value in your available assets. However, a business may be of little value after the death of a principal. In any case, the disposition or conservation of a business interest is a complex matter that should be dealt with in close consultation with the team of professional advisors referred to later in this chapter.

Total Resources

After you have estimated the total death benefits of your life insurance, the value of your Social Security survivors' benefits, and the value of your other assets, add the figures to arrive at the total resources available to your family. Then compare the total resources to the financial requirements of your family; the shortage, if any, is the amount of additional life insurance you need.

If you have never gone through this kind of exercise before, you may be startled by the large amount of additional life insurance you need. This happens frequently, because most people are accustomed to thinking about life insurance in small amounts. For example, $25,000 sounds like a lot of money, but even at 6 percent interest it will provide only about $3,200 per year for ten years.

The important thing to remember is that the purpose of life insurance is to meet the financial objectives you have established. If your objectives are large, a large amount of life insurance may be needed. If you believe the additional amount of life insurance indicated is more than you want to buy or can afford, one possibility is to revise your objectives downward. Another possibility is to leave your objectives unchanged at least for the moment. After you have completed this book, you will have a better idea of what it costs to own life insurance and you can then reconsider your objectives if you still want to do so.

Other Considerations

The discussion in this chapter applies primarily to persons with dependents. If you have no dependents, your basic concern is to assure that the financial resources available at your death are sufficient to cover final expenses and debts, unless you also want to make bequests to relatives, friends, or charities. Beyond these considerations, the primary reason for persons without present dependents to buy life insurance is to put it into effect while they are still in good health and able to qualify easily for it. Then they will be sure to have life insurance later if they need it. At young ages, however, the likelihood is small that a person will become ineligible for life insurance at regular rates within a few years.

It is often said that a person should buy life insurance at a young age because it is cheaper that way. This argument is fallacious. The premiums are smaller when you are younger, but when you are younger there are more years until your death. In computing their premiums, life insurance companies attempt to allocate their expenses and profits equitably among their policyowners. So the age of a newly insured person should be a matter of indifference to the companies and to the policyowner at the time of purchase. In short, it doesn't make much difference when you buy, provided you can qualify at that time.

An important question arises with respect to life insurance on your spouse. If both spouses are gainfully employed, the earnings of each should be considered in determining the life insurance needs of the other. If one spouse is not gainfully employed, the cost of replacing that spouse's duties in the family should be considered in determining the life insurance needs of that spouse.

The financial consequences of the death of a non-wage-earning spouse are sometimes underestimated. In addition to final expenses, the family loses the income tax benefits of the joint return privilege. The family also may incur large expenses if someone has to be hired to take care of the house and children so that the surviving spouse can continue to earn a living. In other words, insurance on the life of a non-wage-earning spouse can be important, although it should be considered of lower priority than adequate insurance on the life of the sole or primary breadwinner. The procedure described in this chapter can be applied to determine an appropriate amount of life insurance for a non-wage-earning spouse.

Another question relates to life insurance on children. Unless a child is an income-producing prodigy, all that needs to be considered are final expenses and assurance that the child will have coverage when he or she needs it. Insurance on children should be considered of even lower priority than insurance on a non-wage-earning spouse.

The discussion in this chapter applies primarily to persons who have not accumulated a substantial amount of wealth and whose incomes are derived mostly from personal efforts. For such persons—the majority of the population—life insurance performs a property-creation function in that existing assets must be supplemented in order to provide adequately for the family after the death of the breadwinner.

The special problems of persons of substantial wealth are beyond the scope of this chapter. For these persons, life insurance may perform a property-conservation function in that life insurance can be used to protect the existing assets from erosion because of death taxes and from asset shrinkage that may accompany forced liquidation. For persons in this category, the help of a team of professional advisors—including an attorney experienced in estate planning, a certified public accountant, an experienced trust officer, and a highly qualified life insurance agent—is essential.

Chapter 3

Major Types of Life Insurance

The number of different types of life insurance contracts on the market is large. Most companies write a dozen or more basic policies and several riders (optional clauses) that may be added to nearly all of the basic policies. The number of possible combinations, therefore, is mind boggling. The effect of this proliferation is confusion and frustration for the buyer.

Fortunately, there is a way out for the consumer. The life insurance needs of almost any buyer can be met with just two policy types—one-year renewable term and straight life—or some of each. This chapter is designed to familiarize you with the major features of these two policy types. Also discussed are two new policy types that may be used in lieu of straight life, and three important riders that may be attached to many basic policies.

Some Terminology

At the outset, a comment on terminology is needed. The "insured" is the person on whose life the policy is issued. The death of the insured is the event that triggers the payment of the policy's death benefit.

The "beneficiary" is the person who receives the policy's death benefit upon the death of the insured. The beneficiary designation is discussed in Chapter 9.

The "policyowner" is the person who possesses the ownership rights in a life insurance policy. One of the ownership rights, for example, is the right to designate the beneficiary. The ownership rights are discussed in Chapter 9. In most cases, the insured and the policyowner are the same person, although there are many situations in which the policy is owned by someone other than the insured. For example, a policy may be owned by the spouse of the insured.

The "premium payer" is the person who pays the premiums. In most cases, the policyowner and the premium payer are the same person, although there are many exceptions. For example, premiums may be paid by the spouse of the policyowner. The payment of premiums does not give rise to ownership rights, and in the example just given the payment of premiums is a gift to the policyowner from the spouse. In the discussion that follows, it is assumed that the policyowner and the premium payer are the same person.

Major Policy Features

To understand any life insurance policy, you must have information on six aspects of the policy: duration, death benefit, premiums, savings component, protection component, and dividends. Each of these items is discussed in this section of the chapter.

Duration

The duration of a life insurance policy is the maximum period of time over which the coverage continues if the insured survives and the policy remains in effect. Almost any duration can be found. There are one-year policies, five-year policies, ten-year policies, twenty-year policies, thirty-year policies, policies that continue to age 65, and policies that continue to age 85. Policies that continue to age 100 are called "whole life" policies, or "life" polices.

Death Benefit

The death benefit of a policy is the amount payable upon the death of the insured. In many types of policies, the death benefit remains constant for the duration of the contract. In some policies, however, the death benefit decreases, and in some policies the death benefit increases. Almost any death benefit pattern is possible.

Premiums

The premium is the amount paid to the insurance company by the premium payer. In some policies, the premium remains constant for the duration of the contract. In some policies, however, the premium increases, and in some policies the premium decreases. Almost any premium pattern is possible.

Premiums may be paid once a year (annually), twice a year (semi-annually), four times a year (quarterly), or twelve times a year (monthly). When premiums are paid other than annually, the insurance company usually imposes carrying charges. This subject is discussed in Chapter 14.

Savings Component

Some life insurance policies provide for a cash value, which is the amount paid to the policyowner when premium payments are discontinued and the policy is surrendered. Such policies are said to contain a savings component. The amount of the cash value is specified in the policy. In many policies, the cash value increases steadily over time. In some policies, however, the cash value increases and then decreases. Many cash-value patterns are possible.

Protection Component

Since the death benefit is payable upon the death of the insured, and since the cash value is available to the policyowner while the insured is alive, the amount of life insurance protection in a policy at any particular time may be viewed as the difference between the death benefit and the cash value at that time. If a policy has a death benefit that is constant and a cash value that is increasing steadily over time, the protection component may be viewed as decreasing steadily over time.

Dividends

Many policies are "participating," which means that the insurance company contemplates the payment of periodic (usually annual) "dividends" to the policyowner. The word "dividend" in this context is a misnomer, because it is different from the typical cash dividend paid to the owner of a share of stock.

The life insurance policy dividend is sometimes considered to be a refund of an overcharge in the premium, a benefit payment provided for in the premium, a share in the earnings of the insurance company, or a combination of these items. You need not be overly concerned about precisely what the dividend is or where it comes from, nor should you be lured into the belief that the dividend is some sort of miracle wrought by the insurance company. You should be concerned mainly about the size of the dividends.

To be in a position to judge the price of a policy, you must have information on the year-by-year dividends. In the case of a newly issued policy, such figures are referred to as "illustrated dividends" or as a "dividend illustration." These phrases mean that the dividends shown will be paid by the company if no future changes are made in the factors entering into the calculation of the dividends. Dividends are not (and cannot be) guaranteed, but rather are subject to change—upward or downward—by the company. Moreover, companies do not "estimate" dividends; instead, they merely "illustrate" what the dividends will be if no changes are made.

In the case of a policy issued years ago, the dividends paid by the company in past years may be listed. Such figures are referred to as "historical dividends" or as a "dividend history."

Some cash-value policies issued today are designated as "nonparticipating." In past years it was adequate to describe a nonparticipating policy as one on which the insurance company does not pay dividends. Today such a description is inadequate, because some nonparticipating policies provide that the company may change the premiums. Also, some nonparticipating policies provide for interest to be credited to the cash value in an amount not specified in the policy. Such policies should be viewed as participating.

One-Year Renewable Term

The one-year renewable term policy, which is sometimes called "yearly renewable term" or "annual renewable term," is a widely offered and widely purchased type of life insurance coverage. It has a duration of one year; however, the word "renewable" means that the protection may be continued for one or more additional one-year periods without requiring the insured to qualify for the insurance upon renewal. In insurance jargon, the policy may be "renewed" for one or more additional one-year periods "without evidence of insurability." The policy specifies either the number of times the policy may be renewed or the age to which it may be renewed. Thus, the policyowner has the option to continue the coverage with no questions asked— even if the insured's health has deteriorated or the insured has entered a hazardous occupation.

The death benefit of a one-year renewable term policy remains constant through its one-year duration. Also, the death benefit usually remains unchanged each time the policy is renewed for an additional one-year term. Each time a one-year renewable term policy is renewed, the premium increases. Furthermore, each increase in premium is likely to be larger than the previous increase. The reason for the increasing premiums is that death rates increase with advancing age.

A one-year renewable term policy has no cash value, and therefore no savings component. Since the amount of life insurance protection in a policy may be viewed as the difference between its death benefit and its cash value, and since a one-year renewable term policy has no cash value, the amount of protection in such a policy is equal to its death benefit. Some one-year renewable term policies are participating, and some are nonparticipating.

Straight Life

The straight life policy, which is sometimes called "ordinary life," is another widely offered and widely purchased type of life insurance coverage. To understand the straight life policy, you must have detailed information on the six aspects of the contract discussed earlier.

The duration of a modern straight life policy is to the insured's age 100. If the insured survives and the policyowner continues paying premiums until the termination of the coverage at age 100, the company will pay the death benefit to the policyowner. In the case of a straight life policy issued at age 35, therefore, the duration of the contract is sixty-five years. The death benefit of a straight life policy remains unchanged for the duration of the contract.

The annual premiums for a straight life policy are the same each year and payable for the duration of the contract. In the jargon of the insurance industry, the straight life policy provides for "level" premiums. The word "payable" means that the premiums may be paid, and if they are, the insurance company must accept them. But the premiums do not have to be paid. The policyowner may decide to discontinue the premiums and receive the cash value of the policy. (Other options that are available to the policyowner are discussed in Chapter 11.) Also, premiums are no longer payable after the insured dies. Although this point may seem obvious, it is mentioned here because of the anecdote about a life insurance company's receipt of the following letter:

> We just received a notice from you that the annual premium on my husband's life insurance policy is due. Unfortunately, we cannot afford to pay it, and must therefore cancel the policy. You see, my husband died seven years ago, and we are having an increasingly difficult time making ends meet.

The cash value of a straight life policy grows steadily larger each year the policy remains in effect. For a $100,000 straight life policy issued at age 35, for example, the cash value may be $5,000 after five years, $12,000 after ten years, $28,000 after twenty years, and $100,000 after sixty-five years. The cash value is equal to the death benefit after sixty-five years because, as noted, if the insured survives to age 100 and the policyowner continues to pay the premiums, the death benefit will be paid to the policyowner.

Because of the sales and administrative expenses associated with the issuance of a new policy, cash values in the first one or two years frequently are zero or small. These expenses are the reason for the "front-end load" in most cash-value policies.

The level-premium arrangement, with its associated cash values, makes established life insurance companies major financial institutions. At the same time, the level-premium arrangement transforms what otherwise would be purely an insurance transaction into a combination or package transaction involving both life insurance protection and a savings component. The characteristics of the savings component are discussed in Chapter 5.

As noted, since the death benefit is payable at the insured's death and the cash value is available to the policyowner during the insured's lifetime, the amount of protection provided by a life insurance policy at any particular time is the difference between the death benefit and the cash value at that time. For example, consider the $100,000 straight life policy referred to earlier. Suppose the policy is now twenty years old, so that its cash value, as mentioned earlier, is $28,000. This figure is the amount available to the policyowner while the insured is alive, and is the amount that should be shown as an asset on the policyowner's personal balance sheet. If the insured dies at this time, the beneficiary will receive the death benefit of $100,000, which exceeds the cash value by $72,000. Because the latter figure is the amount the beneficiary would receive in excess of the amount available to the policyowner while the insured is alive, it should be viewed as the amount of life insurance protection in effect at this time.

The notion that the amount of life insurance protection is the difference between the death benefit and the cash value is based on the premise that the cash value is an asset of the policyowner. The logic of this premise will become evident in Chapter 5, in which the nature of the savings component in cash-value life insurance policies is described.

In a straight life policy, since the cash value grows steadily larger each year the policy remains in force, the amount of life insurance protection becomes steadily smaller. In the $100,000 straight life policy referred to earlier, for example, the amount of life insurance protection would be $95,000 at the end of five years, $88,000 at the end

Figure 1
Diagram of Hypothetical Straight Life Policy

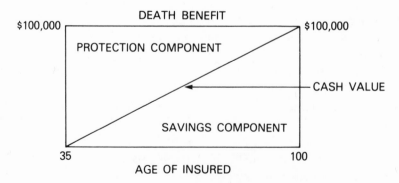

of ten years, $72,000 at the end of twenty years, and zero at the end of sixty-five years.

The relationships among the death benefit, the savings component, and the protection component of a straight life policy issued at age 35 are illustrated in Figure 1. Note that the death benefit is constant for the sixty-five-year policy duration, that the savings component steadily increases, and that the protection component steadily decreases.

Many of the cash-value policies sold today are participating, and some are nonparticipating. When considering a participating policy, it is important to have illustrated dividend figures.

How to Display the Major Policy Features

Figures for the first thirty years of a hypothetical one-year renewable term policy are shown in Table 2. Figures for the first thirty years of a hypothetical straight life policy are shown in Table 3. These tables display the major features of these two policy types and illustrate the basic differences between them.

Note the steadily increasing premiums in the one-year renewable term policy, and the constant premiums in the straight life policy. Note the constant death benefit in both policies. Note the absence of any cash value (savings component) in the one-year renewable term policy, and the steadily increasing cash value in the straight life policy. Note the constant amount of protection in the one-year renewable term policy, and the steadily decreasing amount of protection in the straight life policy. Note the illustrated (nonguaranteed) dividends in both policies.

The figures in Tables 2 and 3 are basic information about any life insurance policy. Chapter 8 explains how such information may be used to determine whether a policy is competitively priced.

Universal Life

Many companies now offer universal life, which is a new type of cash-value life insurance. It has two characteristics that distinguish it from traditional cash-value insurance—flexibility and transparency.

Universal life has flexibility in both premium and death benefit. The premium may be increased or decreased (within limits) by the policyowner. Changing the premium has the effect of speeding up or slowing down the growth of the cash value, or even decreasing the cash value. Also, the death benefit may be increased or decreased

Table 2
Yearly Raw Data for Hypothetical $100,000 Participating One-Year Renewable Term Policy Issued to a Man Aged 35

(1) Year	(2) Age	(3) Annual Premium	(4) Cash Value	(5) Annual Dividend*	(6) Death Benefit	(7) Amount of Protection**
1	35	$ 251	$0	$ 0	$100,000	$100,000
2	36	259	0	0	100,000	100,000
3	37	271	0	56	100,000	100,000
4	38	343	0	60	100,000	100,000
5	39	364	0	64	100,000	100,000
6	40	390	0	69	100,000	100,000
7	41	418	0	75	100,000	100,000
8	42	449	0	81	100,000	100,000
9	43	484	0	88	100,000	100,000
10	44	524	0	95	100,000	100,000
11	45	569	0	104	100,000	100,000
12	46	618	0	114	100,000	100,000
13	47	673	0	124	100,000	100,000
14	48	732	0	136	100,000	100,000
15	49	800	0	149	100,000	100,000
16	50	873	0	163	100,000	100,000
17	51	952	0	179	100,000	100,000
18	52	1,039	0	196	100,000	100,000
19	53	1,131	0	212	100,000	100,000
20	54	1,235	0	233	100,000	100,000
21	55	1,353	0	256	100,000	100,000
22	56	1,485	0	282	100,000	100,000
23	57	1,631	0	310	100,000	100,000
24	58	1,789	0	341	100,000	100,000
25	59	1,966	0	369	100,000	100,000
26	60	2,154	0	391	100,000	100,000
27	61	2,347	0	423	100,000	100,000
28	62	2,562	0	459	100,000	100,000
29	63	2,799	0	496	100,000	100,000
30	64	3,049	0	539	100,000	100,000

*Neither estimates nor guarantees, but merely illustrations of the company's current dividend scale.
**Death benefit (column 6) minus cash value (column 4).

(within limits) by the policyowner. Changing the death benefit also may affect the rate of growth of the cash value. If the death benefit is increased substantially, the company will require the insured to qualify for the increase by furnishing evidence of insurability.

Table 3
Yearly Raw Data for Hypothetical $100,000 Participating Straight Life Policy Issued to a Man Aged 35

(1) Year	(2) Age	(3) Annual Premium	(4) Cash Value	(5) Annual Dividend*	(6) Death Benefit	(7) Amount of Protection**
1	35	$1,500	$ 0	$ 50	$100,000	$100,000
2	36	1,500	1,250	100	100,000	98,750
3	37	1,500	2,500	150	100,000	97,500
4	38	1,500	3,750	200	100,000	96,250
5	39	1,500	5,000	250	100,000	95,000
6	40	1,500	6,400	300	100,000	93,600
7	41	1,500	7,800	350	100,000	92,200
8	42	1,500	9,200	400	100,000	90,800
9	43	1,500	10,600	450	100,000	89,400
10	44	1,500	12,000	500	100,000	88,000
11	45	1,500	13,600	550	100,000	86,400
12	46	1,500	15,200	600	100,000	84,800
13	47	1,500	16,800	650	100,000	83,200
14	48	1,500	18,400	700	100,000	81,600
15	49	1,500	20,000	750	100,000	80,000
16	50	1,500	21,600	800	100,000	78,400
17	51	1,500	23,200	850	100,000	76,800
18	52	1,500	24,800	900	100,000	75,200
19	53	1,500	26,400	950	100,000	73,600
20	54	1,500	28,000	1,000	100,000	72,000
21	55	1,500	29,600	1,050	100,000	70,400
22	56	1,500	31,200	1,100	100,000	68,800
23	57	1,500	32,800	1,150	100,000	67,200
24	58	1,500	34,400	1,200	100,000	65,600
25	59	1,500	36,000	1,250	100,000	64,000
26	60	1,500	37,600	1,300	100,000	62,400
27	61	1,500	39,200	1,350	100,000	60,800
28	62	1,500	40,800	1,400	100,000	59,200
29	63	1,500	42,400	1,450	100,000	57,600
30	64	1,500	44,000	1,500	100,000	56,000

*Neither estimates nor guarantees, but merely illustrations of the company's current dividend scale.
**Death benefit (column 6) minus cash value (column 4).

Universal life has transparency in that the policy is broken down (the word in the insurance jargon is "unbundled") into its protection, savings, and expense components. When the policyowner pays a premium, the insurance company takes out an expense charge and adds the remainder to the cash value. The company takes out of the cash value a "mortality charge" (and perhaps an additional expense charge) to pay for the life insurance protection, and adds interest to the remaining cash value. The policy resembles a combination of one-year renewable term and a savings account.

If you consider buying a universal life policy, you should obtain figures based upon the assumption you will pay premiums that approximate those of a straight life policy for the same death benefit issued at the same age. The figures can then be displayed as shown in Table 3. The only difference is that usually dividends are not listed; rather, all of the interest (including the interest that is illustrated and not guaranteed) is included in the cash-value figures. Also, you should follow the procedure described in Chapter 8 to determine whether the charges built into the policy are reasonable.

Be sure to obtain from the company a written explanation of the federal income tax treatment of universal life. This is important because, under current tax laws, it is possible for the death benefit of a universal life policy to be disqualified as life insurance for federal income tax purposes. The result would be some unexpected income taxes for your beneficiary upon your death.

Also, you should request an agreement from the company to reimburse your beneficiary for any extra taxes that have to be paid as a result of the company's error. For example, one way for the death benefit of a universal life policy to be disqualified as life insurance for federal income tax purposes is for you to pay too large a premium relative to the policy's death benefit. The rules for determining what constitutes "too large a premium" are complex, and the companies selling universal life are creating systems to prevent such an occurrence. If a company's system breaks down, however, it may be your beneficiary who suffers the consequences. This is why you should request a reimbursement agreement from the company.*

Adjustable Life

A few companies offer adjustable life, which is another relatively new type of cash-value life insurance. It may be distinguished from traditional cash-value life insurance because of its flexibility; it resembles

---

*The word "request" was used in this discussion because you should not necessarily refuse to buy a universal life policy if the company denies your request for a reimbursement agreement. But you should make the request. If enough consumers do so, the companies will be made to realize that consumers are concerned about the problem.

universal life in that respect. However, it does not possess the transparency of universal life; in that respect it resembles traditional cash-value life insurance. If you consider buying an adjustable life policy, you should obtain illustrative figures based upon the assumption you will pay premiums sufficient to maintain the policy in the form of straight life. The figures can then be displayed as shown in Table 3.

Three Important Riders

This section describes three important riders—the waiver-of-premium rider, the accidental-death rider, and the guaranteed-insurability rider. They may be attached to many basic policy types, and should be considered when you buy life insurance.

Waiver of Premium

A waiver-of-premium rider usually provides that premiums are waived if the insured becomes totally disabled before some specified age—such as 65—and if the disability lasts more than six months. The word "waived" means that the premiums do not have to be paid by the policyowner, but the policy is treated as though the premiums are being paid. When the insured has been totally disabled for six months, the usual waiver-of-premium rider makes the waiver retroactive to the beginning of the disability; thus any premiums paid by the policyowner during the first six months of the disability would be refunded by the company.

This rider is a form of disability insurance. During the continuance of the disability, the premiums are waived and the various benefits provided in the contract (including the death benefit, the cash values, and the dividends) continue as though premiums were being paid by the policyowner. When the disability ends, the policyowner resumes premium payments and has no liability for repayment of the waived premiums.

The definition of the phrase "totally disabled" varies among companies, but a common definition provides that the insured is totally disabled if he or she is unable, because of an illness or injury, to perform any of the duties of his or her regular occupation. Many companies apply this type of definition to the first few years of a disability, and then apply a stricter definition to a disability that continues beyond the initial period. For example, after the first few years of disability, an insured might be considered "totally disabled" if he or she is unable to perform any of the duties of his or her regular occupation, or any other occupation for which he or she is fitted as a result of education, training, and experience.

A few companies include the waiver-of-premium rider in their contracts "without specific extra charge." Most companies, however, impose a specific charge for the rider. To examine the cost of the waiver-of-premium rider, express the annual cost of the rider as a percentage of the annual premium with the cost of the rider included, because the full premium, including the cost of the rider, would be waived in the event of a disability. For example, if the annual premium for the life insurance is $1,600 and the rider costs $45, the cost of the rider is 2.7 percent ($45 divided by $1,645).

If you are buying a term policy and contemplating the addition of a waiver-of-premium rider, the comparison problem is difficult. Waiver-of-premium riders available for term policies differ widely among companies; a low-priced rider may be a restrictive one. The waiver-of-premium rider as it relates to term policies is discussed in Chapter 10.

It is often a good idea to add the waiver-of-premium rider when you buy a life insurance policy. The need for it depends on the extent of your disability insurance program, and many people have inadequate protection against disability. The waiver-of-premium rider is particularly important in the case of a large policy, because a large premium would be a burden in the event of a serious, long-term disability.

Some companies will attach to a life insurance policy a rider providing for both waiver of premium and payment of a monthly income in the event that the insured becomes totally disabled as the result of an illness or injury. This type of disability-income rider should be analyzed as though it were a separate disability-income policy. The subject of disability-income insurance is a part of the extensive subject of health insurance and is beyond the scope of this book.

Accidental Death
Nearly all life insurance companies will attach to a basic life insurance policy a rider often called "double indemnity." This rider provides an additional death benefit, usually equal to the benefit provided in the basic policy, if the insured's death results from an accident which occurs prior to a specified age such as 65 or 70.

The premium for an accidental-death benefit may seem small, but most deaths do not qualify for accidental-death benefits. Automobile accidents are spectacular and often make the newspaper front pages, but they are far outnumbered by the more obscure notices on the obituary pages. Accidental-death insurance is difficult to justify on rational grounds. Why should you provide more protection for your family if you die in an automobile (or any other) accident than if you die of a heart attack? Indeed, if a differentiation is to be made, it would be logical to provide more protection in the event of a non-accidental death, because a long illness preceding such a death might leave the family in more difficult financial circumstances than a sudden death from an accident.

If you conscientiously measure your life insurance needs, using the procedure outlined in Chapter 2, and if you buy life insurance accordingly, you need not buy accidental-death coverage. Nor should you buy other more limited forms of life insurance, such as the air trip coverage available at airports.* Should you decide to buy accidental-death insurance, however, be sure to read the definition of accidental death in the contract, paying particular attention to the various exclusions from coverage.

Guaranteed Insurability

Many companies will attach to a life insurance policy a rider that permits the policyowner to purchase additional life insurance at certain specified future dates without evidence of insurability. A guaranteed-insurability rider specifies the dates on which the policyowner may purchase additional life insurance with no questions asked. For example, the dates might be the policy anniversaries nearest the insured's twenty-fifth, twenty-eighth, thirty-first, thirty-fourth, thirty-seventh, and fortieth birthdays. Thus, the older the insured when the original policy is applied for, the fewer options the policyowner will have, and the rider may not be available if the insured is beyond age 37 when the original policy is applied for.

The maximum amount of additional life insurance that can be purchased on any option date usually is called the "option amount" and is

---

*Air trip coverage should be frowned upon as an invitation to a desperate person who might carry a bomb aboard a passenger airplane for the purpose of benefiting his or her family financially. Air trip coverage would be prohibited if the Air Line Pilots Association had its way.

specified in the policy. On any option date, the policyowner may exercise the option in full or in part, or may pass. Usually the options are not cumulative. Thus, an option once passed is lost forever, but later options are still available.

Major differences are found in the riders offered by various companies. For example, one of the most significant questions is whether the waiver-of-premium rider may be included without evidence of insurability in a policy purchased through the exercise of an option.

The premium for the additional life insurance purchased under an option is governed by the age of the insured at the option date. Thus the advantage of the rider is not premium savings, but rather that no evidence of insurability will be required. The guaranteed-insurability rider should be considered by or for young people who have reason to believe they will be adding to their life insurance from time to time.

Chapter 4

Other Types of
Life Insurance

This chapter describes several types of life insurance other than those discussed in the preceding chapter. Because of the large variety of available policies and riders, the material presented is not exhaustive. However, it does touch on the most widely sold forms of coverage.

Since your needs can be met with the major types of policies described in Chapter 3, this chapter is included primarily for reference purposes. You may want to familiarize yourself with these additional types of life insurance, or you may have previously purchased one or more of them.

Other Types of Term Policies

One-year renewable term life insurance was described in Chapter 3. In this section, several other types of term life insurance are described.

Level Term

The word "term" refers to life insurance coverage that terminates without cash value at the end of a specified number of years or at a specified age. The word "level," when used with the word "term," means that the death benefit does not change for the duration of the coverage. One-year renewable term is an example of level term coverage. The death benefit remains the same during the one-year term of the coverage, and the insurance terminates at the end of the year without cash value; however, the policyowner may renew the coverage for successive one-year terms at higher premiums with no questions asked.

Another example of level term insurance is five-year renewable term. The death benefit is the same for five years, and the premium is the same for five years. The insurance terminates at the end of five years without cash value; however, the policyowner may renew the coverage for successive five-year terms at higher premiums with no questions asked.

Many level term policies are not renewable; they expire at the end of the coverage period without cash value, and the policyowner must apply for a new policy to retain the original amount of coverage. To do so, the insured must still be able to qualify. One-year nonrenewable, five-year nonrenewable, and ten-year nonrenewable term policies are examples of nonrenewable term coverage. Avoid such policies. You may be nearly certain that a need for life insurance coverage is temporary, but a coronary can change your mind quickly. A renewable term policy costs more than a similar nonrenewable term policy, but the renewal privilege is worth the extra cost.*

Other examples of level term insurance are fifteen-year term, twenty-year term, and term to age 65. These policies usually are nonrenewable. Also, premiums generally remain the same for the

---

*The way to determine the amount of the extra cost is to compare policies issued by the same company. This is often not possible, however, because many companies do not offer renewable and nonrenewable term policies that are otherwise identical.

duration of the coverage. Other things equal, the longer the term, the higher the premium. Indeed, straight life may be viewed as term to age 100, with the proviso that an insured who survives to 100 is considered dead at that time so that the policyowner is eligible to receive the policy's death benefit.

Level term insurance is available not only in separate policies but also in riders that may be attached to a basic policy such as straight life. The advantage of a level term rider, as contrasted with a separate level term policy, is that it is less expensive for a company to issue a rider than to issue a separate policy. These savings may result in a lower cost to the policyowner. Unfortunately, because many companies do not offer separate term policies directly comparable to their term riders, it is often difficult to determine whether such savings are passed on to policyowners. Moreover, the renewal and conversion privileges (discussed in Chapter 10) in term riders sometimes are not as liberal as those found in separate term policies.

Decreasing Term

In decreasing term insurance, the death benefit declines steadily until it reaches zero at expiration. Sometimes the decreases occur annually and sometimes monthly. Premiums usually remain the same and are payable either for the duration of the coverage or for a shorter period. With some companies, for example, the premiums for twenty-year decreasing term are payable for sixteen years.

The coverage may continue for a specified number of years or to a specified age. Examples are ten-year decreasing term, twenty-year decreasing term, and decreasing term to age 65. Straight life may be viewed as a combination of decreasing term to age 100 and an increasing savings component with the sum of the two parts always equal to the death benefit of the straight life policy.

Decreasing term coverage, particularly for thirty years or less, is widely purchased. One reason may be that a large amount of protection is provided initially for a small premium; however, such coverage has important drawbacks.

The protection decreases rapidly, and this decrease can be an important disadvantage. If your health suddenly deteriorates, you may decide you do not want your life insurance protection to decline rapidly. In a level term contract, such as one-year renewable term, you can reduce the protection if you want to do so, but the protection remains level unless you take action to reduce it. And in straight life policies, although the protection declines, the decrease is slower than that usually found in decreasing term coverage, and the protection does not disappear until the insured reaches age 100.

It is sometimes said that a person's need for life insurance tends to decline as the family grows older, because of the decrease in the length of time over which income will be needed in the event of the breadwinner's death. This line of reasoning is used as an argument in favor of decreasing term insurance. Such reasoning, however, does not always apply. Although there may be a decline in the length of the period over which income is needed after the insured's death, there also may be an increase in the desired level of income because of the family's steadily improving standard of living. The increase in the desired level of income may more than offset the decrease in the length of time over which the income is needed. Thus a person's life insurance needs may increase for many years before beginning to decrease.

Another important problem in some decreasing term coverage is found in the conversion clause (discussed in Chapter 10). Some contracts provide that you may exchange the decreasing term coverage for a straight life or other cash-value policy with no questions asked, but the death benefit of the converted policy may not exceed, say, 80 percent of the amount of decreasing term insurance in effect at the time of conversion.

For example, suppose you become seriously ill, drastically altering your insurability status. If you have decreasing term insurance with an 80 percent conversion clause, you will be faced with a dilemma. If you convert, you instantly lose one-fifth of your present coverage. On the other hand, if you do not convert, both the insurance and your conversion privilege will continue to decrease rapidly. If you consider the purchase of decreasing term insurance, examine the conversion clause and avoid those that provide less than 100 percent conversion of the amount of insurance in effect at the time of conversion.

Decreasing term insurance is available with many companies either in separate policies or as riders to be attached to a basic policy such as straight life. Frequently, however, the coverage is available under another name, such as "family income" or "mortgage insurance."

A family-income benefit, which is usually a rider to a basic policy, provides for the payment of a specified monthly income in addition to the death benefit of the basic contract. In a twenty-year family-income arrangement, for example, a monthly income is payable from the insured's death for the remainder of twenty years measured from the policy's issue date. Thus the longer the insured lives, the fewer are the number of income payments. Hence, twenty-year decreasing term coverage is needed to provide the income payments.

An examination of a family-income rider is needed to determine the exact amount of decreasing term coverage provided. Also, it is important that the beneficiary be given the option to take a single-sum settlement instead of the family-income benefit, if the policyowner wants the beneficiary to have that option. Some policies, unless specifically modified to the contrary, provide that the beneficiary must take the specified monthly income payments.

Mortgage insurance usually is decreasing term coverage under which the amount of protection is designed to parallel the declining unpaid balance of a mortgage. Such insurance is sometimes offered as a separate policy and sometimes as a rider to a basic policy such as straight life.

Increasing Term

Increasing term coverage is issued either as a rider to a basic policy, such as straight life, or as a part of a package policy. Most commonly, the coverage is called either a "return-of-premium benefit" or a "return-of-cash-value benefit." Frequently these benefits are limited to twenty years.

For example, a twenty-year return-of-premium benefit provides that the simple total of the premiums paid by the policyowner is paid to the beneficiary in addition to the death benefit of the basic policy in the event of the insured's death during the first twenty years of the policy. The longer the insured lives (up to twenty years), the more is paid at death under the return-of-premium benefit. Hence, twenty-year increasing term coverage is needed to provide the benefit.

A return-of-premium benefit fits nicely into a sales presentation. It can be made to sound like a bargain, or as though the insurance company provides the benefit gratuitously. But the benefit costs money, and the policyowner pays for it.

A twenty-year return-of-cash-value benefit operates in a similar manner. It provides that the cash value of the basic policy is paid to the beneficiary in addition to the death benefit in the event of the insured's death during the first twenty years of the policy. The longer the insured lives (up to twenty years), the more is paid at death under the return-of-cash-value benefit. Hence, twenty-year increasing term coverage is needed to provide the benefit.

The return-of-cash-value benefit also fits well into sales presentations. Some critics of the life insurance business argue that a conventional straight life policy "should" pay the cash value to the beneficiary in addition to the death benefit at the insured's death. The argument has no basis in fact and arises from a lack of understanding of life insurance arithmetic. The return-of-cash-value benefit allows the insurance company to meet the objections of these critics. However, the benefit costs money, and the policyowner pays for it.

Front-End-Loaded Term

As mentioned in Chapter 3, the cash values of straight life policies in the first one or two years frequently are zero or quite small because of the sales and administrative expenses associated with the issuance of new policies. These expenses are the reason for the "front-end load" in cash-value policies. As explained in Chapter 8, the front-end load in cash-value policies usually is evidenced by yearly prices that are high in the first one or two years relative to the prices in subsequent years.

In a typical one-year renewable term policy, on the other hand, the premium increases each year upon renewal. Since the policy contains no cash values, the yearly prices parallel the premiums, and there is no front-end load comparable to that found in the typical straight life policy. Because of the absence of a front-end load in the typical one-year renewable term policy, an insurance company cannot pay its agent as much first-year commission as that associated with the sale of a straight life policy, unless the company is willing and able to use accumulated resources. Thus agents may sell large amounts of one-year renewable term but still fail to earn enough commissions to survive in the business.

Some companies, in an effort to stimulate their agents to sell term insurance, have developed various forms of front-end-loaded term insurance. In such policies, the premium in the first year is larger than in the first year of a typical one-year renewable term policy. Unfortunately, efforts to sell such policies often include certain kinds of deceptive sales practices whose objective is to obscure the front-end load. The most prominent of such policies in recent years has been the "deposit term policy," in which the sales presentation places the emphasis on the "deposit" (which is not a deposit) and distracts the buyer from the fact that the policy is front-end loaded.

To put it bluntly, a consumer has no reason to buy a front-end-loaded term policy when there are conventional term policies available without a front-end load. If you follow the procedure outlined in Chapter 8, you will have no difficulty in avoiding front-end-loaded term products.

Other Types of Whole Life Policies

As mentioned earlier, the duration of modern whole life policies is to age 100. The straight life policy, which is a whole life policy, was described in Chapter 3. In this section, certain other types of whole life policies are discussed.

Limited-Payment Life

A limited-payment life policy is similar to a straight life policy in that the duration of the contract is to age 100 (in the case of modern policies) and the death benefit remains the same for the duration of the contract. It differs from a straight life policy, however, in that the premiums are payable over a time period shorter than the duration of the contract.

The premiums for a limited-payment life policy usually are level during the premium-paying period, and are larger than the premiums for a corresponding straight life policy. The savings component grows more rapidly during the premium-paying period, and therefore the protection component declines more rapidly than in a straight life policy.

Some limited-payment life policies have premiums payable for a specified number of years. Examples are thirty-payment life (in which premiums are payable for thirty years), twenty-payment life, fifteen-payment life, and ten-payment life. The extreme case is single-premium life, in which one premium is paid.

Some limited-payment life policies have premiums payable to a specified age. Examples are life paid up at age 60 (often called "life 60"), life 65, and so on. When premiums are payable to an advanced age, such as 85, 90, or 95, the premiums and cash values closely resemble those of straight life (in which premiums are payable to age

100), and some companies offer such policies instead of straight life.

At the end of the premium-paying period, a policy is said to be "paid up," meaning that no more premiums are needed. The cash value at that time, however, does not equal the death benefit. The cash value equals the policy's death benefit only at age 100. This point is illustrated in Figure 2, which is a simplified diagram of a twenty-payment life policy issued at age 35. After the premium-paying period, interest earnings on the savings component pay for the continuing cost of the protection and also cause the cash value to increase, although at a slower rate than during the premium-paying period.

Figure 2
Diagram of Hypothetical Twenty-Payment Life Policy

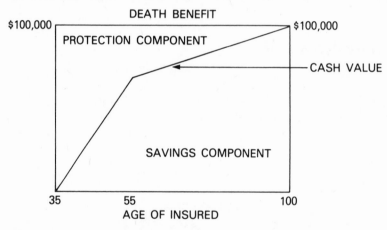

Limited-payment life has two advantages for the buyer. First, the policyowner "gets rid of the obligation to pay premiums." Second, the savings component grows more rapidly during the premium-paying period than in straight life.

Offsetting these advantages are four disadvantages. First, during the premium-paying period the premiums for limited-payment life are larger than the premiums for straight life. Second, the protection component declines more rapidly during the premium-paying period than in straight life. Third, although premiums for limited-payment life are no longer payable after the premium-paying period, the policyowner continues to be charged, because a portion of the interest earnings on the savings component of the "paid-up" policy is used to pay for the continuing protection. Fourth, evidence suggests that many companies charge more for the protection in limited-payment life than for the protection in straight life.*

Modified Life

A modified life policy is a whole life policy in which the premium schedule is modified from that of the typical straight life policy. For example, in a modified-three policy the premiums are level for the first three years, after which they increase and then remain at the higher level in subsequent years. In a modified-five policy, the premiums increase to their ultimate level after five years. In a modified-five-and-ten policy, the premiums increase after five years and then increase again after five more years before reaching their ultimate level.

Modified life policies can be used as the basis for an attractive sales presentation. For example, lower premiums in the early years can be made to seem attractive as an incentive for you to start your life insurance program. The fact is, however, that greater flexibility can be achieved—frequently at less cost—through the use of one-year renewable term, or a combination of one-year renewable term and straight life. For example, a modified-five policy requires a premium increase after five years; however, if you buy one-year renewable term, you can convert part or all of the coverage to straight life (thus increasing your premiums) whenever it is convenient for you to do so.

Modified life policies may also involve premiums in the early years that are higher than subsequent premiums. For example, a modified-one policy may have a higher premium in the first year than in subsequent years. This type of policy is sometimes used with a rider providing that, if the policyowner continues paying premiums at the first-year level, the difference in the second and subsequent years will go into a savings accumulation.

Endowment Policies

Many varieties of endowment policies are written. This section describes only conventional and retirement income endowments.

---

*Joseph M. Belth, *The Retail Price Structure in American Life Insurance* (Bloomington, IN: Indiana University School of Business, 1966), pp. 87–95.

Conventional Endowments

An endowment policy is one in which the cash value equals the death benefit at the end of the policy's duration.* Some endowments are for a specified number of years; the thirty-year endowment, the twenty-year endowment, and the ten-year endowment are examples. Other endowments are written to a specified age; the endowment at age 60 and the endowment at age 65 are examples.

Endowment policies usually have a level death benefit and level premiums for the duration of the contract.** In this sense, a straight life policy may be viewed as an endowment at age 100. When an endowment period extends to an advanced age, such as 85, 90, or 95, the premiums and cash values resemble those of straight life, and some companies offer such policies instead of straight life.

An endowment has the advantage of a rapidly growing savings component. Offsetting this advantage are large premiums (the shorter the endowment period, the larger the premiums) and a rapidly declining protection component. The most serious drawback of a short-term endowment, such as a twenty-year endowment, is that the contract terminates and the protection ends at a time when the policy-owner may still need continued protection. Figure 3 is a simplified diagram of a twenty-year endowment.

Retirement Income Endowments

A retirement income endowment (sometimes called an "income endowment" or "retirement income" policy) is designed to generate a large enough cash value to produce a specified life income beginning at a given age. Such a policy could be called a "super endowment" because the cash value in the later years exceeds the original death benefit. Frequently the income provided is $10 per month for each $1,000 of the policy's initial death benefit. A $50,000 retirement income endowment at age 65, for example, may generate a cash value of about $80,000, which is the approximate amount needed to provide a life income of $500 per month for a man beginning at age 65. The premiums usually are level for the duration of the contract.

---

*A semi-endowment policy is one in which the cash value equals half the death benefit at the end of the policy's duration.

**Exceptions are limited-payment endowments. A twenty-payment endowment at age 65 issued at age 35, for example, has a thirty-year duration, but premiums are payable for only twenty years.

Figure 3
Diagram of Hypothetical Twenty-Year Endowment

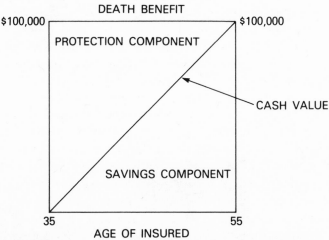

If the insured dies before the age at which the income commences, the beneficiary receives the initial death benefit or the cash value, whichever is larger. If the insured survives to the age at which the income commences, the policyowner usually has the option to be paid the specified income, to receive the cash value in a single sum, or to select any of the other settlement options (discussed in Chapter 9) provided in the contract. If the policyowner chooses to receive the funds in installments, the amount payable to the beneficiary at the subsequent death of the insured will depend upon the provisions of the particular income arrangement chosen by the policyowner.

The retirement income endowment has the advantage of a rapidly growing savings component. Offsetting this advantage are high premiums and a rapidly declining protection component. Indeed, since the amount payable to the beneficiary in the event of the insured's death during the later years of the policy equals the cash value, no life insurance protection is provided during that period. In short, during the early policy years a retirement income endowment is like a short-term endowment; during the later policy years it is solely a savings plan providing no life insurance protection. Figure 4 is a simplified diagram of a retirement income endowment at age 65.

Multi-Life Policies

Up to this point, all the coverages described are single-life contracts;

Figure 4
Diagram of Hypothetical Retirement Income Endowment at Age 65

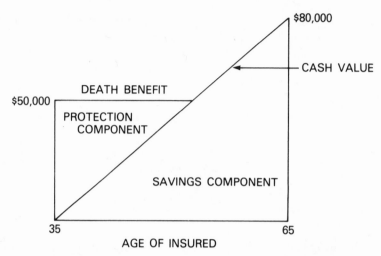

that is, they are based on one life. Some life insurance policies, however, cover more than one life.

Family Policies

Family policies are sold in "units." One unit may consist of $5,000
of straight life on the husband, $2,000 of term to age 65 on the wife,
and $1,000 of term to age 25 on each of the children. The $1,000 of
term coverage on a child usually is convertible to $5,000 of straight
life without evidence of insurability when the child reaches age 25.

A family policy is a convenient way to insure the lives of all members of a family. But it is a complex arrangement. The complexity
becomes apparent when the policy is examined with regard to situations such as the following: the husband dies and the wife remarries;
the wife dies and the husband remarries; or the husband and wife are
divorced and each remarry.

Economies may be realized because it is less expensive for an insurance company to cover several persons in one policy than to issue
separate policies. However, if you determine your life insurance
needs in accordance with the procedure described in Chapter 2, you
probably will require separate policies to obtain the appropriate
amounts of life insurance. Furthermore, separate policies are easier
to modify as changes occur in your family status. For these reasons,
confine your purchases to single-life policies.

Joint Life

Another example of a policy covering more than one life is the joint-life contract. Such a policy covers two lives—most frequently either husband and wife or two business partners—and the death benefit is payable upon the first death. Such policies often contain a conversion clause allowing the survivor to buy a new policy on his or her own life without evidence of insurability within a specified time after the first death.

A variation on the joint-life policy is the last-survivor contract. Such a policy covers two lives and the death benefit is payable upon the second death. Last-survivor policies are sold in most instances because of the likelihood of greater death taxes when the surviving spouse dies than when the first one dies.

The premium for a joint-life policy is smaller than the combined premiums for policies with the same death benefit on each life separately. The premium for a last-survivor policy is even smaller. The problem is the difficulty of determining whether the price of a joint-life or a last-survivor policy is reasonable.

You may want to purchase a joint-life or a last-survivor policy. Proceed with caution, however, because the policy you consider may or may not be reasonably priced. No system for determining the reasonableness of the price of a joint-life or a last-survivor policy has yet been published.

Variable Life Insurance

Several companies now offer variable life insurance policies. In these policies, the cash value fluctuates in accordance with the investment performance of an account consisting usually of equity-type assets such as common stocks. The death benefit also fluctuates, but usually is subject to a minimum guaranteed figure. Anyone interested in a variable life policy can obtain an elaborate prospectus.

Many companies are planning to introduce a new type of coverage called "flexible premium variable life" insurance. These policies will combine certain characteristics of universal life and variable life. As in universal life (discussed in Chapter 3), the premiums and death benefits will be flexible. As in variable life, the death benefit will fluctuate in accordance with the performance of an account, although the death benefit may or may not be subject to a minimum guaranteed figure. And as in variable life, the cash value will fluctuate in accordance with the performance of an account.

In 1983, the life insurance industry requested certain exemptions from the Investment Company Act of 1940 for flexible premium variable life insurance. Late in 1984, the Securities and Exchange Commission adopted a temporary rule permitting life insurance companies to offer such coverage, and requested public comment on the rule.*

The buyer of a variable life policy based on the performance of a common stock portfolio is assuming investment risk. The size of the death benefit is determined in part by the level of stock prices when the insured dies, and the size of the cash value is determined in part by the level of stock prices when the policy is surrendered.

If you are willing to assume the investment risk, you may want to consider the purchase of a variable life policy. Before you make such a purchase, however, follow the procedure described in Chapter 8 to determine whether the charges built into the policy are reasonable.

Specialty Policies

Some contracts involve a basic policy and several riders combined to fit an elaborate sales presentation. These policies, often called "specialty policies" (they are called "gimmick policies" by their detractors), are so complex that meaningful analysis and understanding of the package are difficult.

The basic policy may be a twenty-payment endowment at age 65. Added to the basic policy may be an increasing term rider to provide a return-of-premium benefit, a rider to provide for savings accumulation in addition to the cash value of the basic policy, and a decreasing term rider to provide a family-income benefit. The result of such a combination may resemble the protection-savings mix of a straight life policy. The moral of the illustration is that some of the complex combinations of coverages are unnecessary and serve only to confuse the consumer.

Some writers have suggested that such policies should be banned from the market by the state insurance commissioners.** Unfortunately, however, no reliable formula is available for distinguishing precisely between specialty policies and conventional policies. Some specialty policies may be reasonably priced, and some con-

---

*See *Federal Register*, December 3, 1984, pp. 47208–47228.

**Spencer L. Kimball and Jon S. Hanson, "The Regulation of Specialty Policies in Life Insurance," *Michigan Law Review*, Vol. LXII (1963–64), pp. 255–256.

ventional policies are not reasonably priced. Disclosure of prices is preferable to prohibition. If prices were made known to buyers, those specialty policies that are high-priced—along with high-priced conventional policies—would tend to disappear from the market.

Industrial Life Insurance

This book deals primarily with ordinary life insurance. The word "ordinary" in this context refers to the type of life insurance in which policies usually have a death benefit of at least $1,000, and in which premiums other than the first are paid by mail annually, semiannually, quarterly, or monthly.

In contrast, the word "industrial" refers to the type of life insurance in which policies usually have a death benefit smaller than $1,000, and in which premiums are collected at the homes of policyowners monthly or weekly. Industrial life insurance is sometimes referred to as "debit life insurance" (because the territory given to an agent who collects premiums is called a "debit") or as "home service life insurance."

Industrial life insurance usually is sold to low-income persons who need the discipline of frequent premium collection at the home. It is sometimes said that many persons would not have any life insurance at all if it were not for industrial life insurance.

The small size of industrial policies and the home collection feature make this form of life insurance expensive. It is unfortunate that high prices must be paid by those who can least afford them. Do not buy industrial life insurance.

Chapter 5

The Savings Component in Cash-Value Life Insurance

As noted in Chapter 3, the life insurance needs of nearly all buyers can be met satisfactorily with one-year renewable term, straight life, or some of each. Once you have determined your life insurance needs, along the lines discussed in Chapter 2, you should decide how much (if any) of those needs you want to meet with straight life (or some other type of cash-value life insurance such as universal life or adjustable life). Then the remainder of your needs can be met with one-year renewable term.

To decide how much straight life to buy (if any), ask yourself how much you want to invest per year in the savings component of cash-value life insurance. The key to making a sound decision about the type of life insurance to buy, therefore, is an understanding of the nature of the savings component in a cash-value life insurance policy. Unfortunately, however, no area of life insurance has been subjected to more double-talk, half-truths, and outright falsehoods.

Some individuals would have you believe that cash values constitute the finest savings device ever conceived. Some of these individuals use deception to show high rates of return on the savings component of cash-value life insurance.*

On the other hand, some individuals would have you believe that cash values constitute the greatest fraud ever perpetrated on consumers. Some of these individuals use deception to show high prices for the protection component of cash-value life insurance.**

Some proponents of cash-value life insurance suggest that no one should buy one-year renewable term. On the other hand, some opponents of cash-value life insurance suggest that no one should buy anything other than one-year renewable term. In recent years, some opponents of cash-value life insurance have been suggesting that no one should buy anything other than term insurance with a front-end load, the chief purpose of which is to provide large commissions to the salesperson and others in the sales organization. Little wonder, then, that cash values are misunderstood by the buying public caught in the middle of these conflicting views.

The truth lies between the extreme positions. Cash values can be useful for those who understand them and want to use them. To decide whether to buy cash-value life insurance and, if so, what proportion of your life insurance needs should be met with such insurance, you need to understand the characteristics of cash values.

This chapter covers eight important aspects of the savings component of cash-value life insurance: its fixed-dollar nature, rates of

---

*One individual used a figure of 44.3 percent, when a properly calculated figure was 3.8 percent. For an explanation, see Joseph M. Belth, "Deceptive Sales Practices in the Life Insurance Business," *Journal of Risk and Insurance*, Vol. XLI, No. 2 (June, 1974), pp. 306–308.

**One individual used a figure of $173.60, when a properly calculated figure was $8.93. For an explanation, see Joseph M. Belth, "How Not To Sell Term Insurance," *The Insurance Forum*, Vol. 5, No. 1 (January, 1978), pp. 1–2.

return, income tax consequences, liquidity, safety, the notion of "forced savings," protection from creditors, and life annuity rates.

Fixed Dollars

The savings component of cash-value life insurance is a fixed-dollar savings medium. The dollar amount of the accumulation is specified in advance, without regard to what those dollars will buy. Proponents of cash values describe them as guaranteed by the issuing company. Opponents of cash values describe them as subject to erosion by inflation. Both descriptions are accurate, and apply generally to fixed-dollar savings media.

Other major savings media that resemble cash values in this respect are bank savings accounts, savings and loan accounts, credit union share accounts, and United States savings bonds. Long-term debt instruments, such as government bonds, corporate bonds, and mortgages, usually are classified as fixed-dollar devices, but these securities are subject to interim market value fluctuations as market interest rates fluctuate. In this sense, long-term debt instruments differ fundamentally from life insurance cash values, which do not fluctuate as market interest rates change.

Such media as common stocks and real estate are equity investments, in the sense that their values are determined by current market conditions; their long-term values are not specified in advance. Equity investments, therefore, differ fundamentally from the savings component of conventional cash-value life insurance policies.

Rates of Return

Opponents of cash-value life insurance usually assert that the savings component generates low rates of return. Although such individuals frequently state that the rate of return is between 2 percent and 4 percent, these figures often are incorrect.

One of the sources of these incorrect figures is found in the "fine print" of life insurance contracts. Shown there are the interest rates used in calculating policy reserves and cash values. Policy reserves are the main liabilities of a life insurance company and are used in measuring the solvency position of the company; they relate to the rate of return on the savings component only indirectly. Cash values represent the savings component, but in order to determine the rate of return on the savings component from the policyowner's point of view, other factors—such as premiums and dividends—must be considered. In nonparticipating policies, on which dividends are not paid, an interest rate higher than the one used in determining cash values frequently is used in determining premiums. In participating policies, an interest rate higher than the one used in determining cash values frequently is used in determining dividends. In short, the interest rates mentioned in the policy contract are not indicative of the rate of return on the savings component.

Proponents of cash-value life insurance, on the other hand, sometimes assert that the savings component generates high rates of return. The deceptive sales practices used to arrive at such figures are complex, but an analogy may help you understand the nature of the problem.

Suppose that you put $1,000 into a savings account at the beginning of each year for ten years, and that the account is credited each year with 6 percent interest. You will end the ninth year with $12,181, and you will add $1,000 to it at the beginning of the tenth year. At the end of the tenth year, your account will be credited with interest of $791 (6 percent of $13,181), making your account balance $13,972 at the end of the tenth year.

Suppose someone told you that you were earning 79.1 percent interest on your tenth-year deposit of $1,000! The problem here stems from a misallocation of the interest, in this case all of it allocated to the tenth-year deposit of $1,000. (Only $60 of the interest should have been allocated to the tenth-year deposit of $1,000, and the other $731 of interest should have been allocated to the deposits made in the preceding years.) This kind of misallocation is used in some life insurance sales presentations. But the error is not nearly as evident, because of the complexity of the life insurance contract and the complexity of life insurance sales presentations.

Another way proponents of cash-value life insurance frequently overstate the rate of return on the savings component is to put the emphasis on the gross interest rate while either ignoring or downplaying the expense charges. This practice is particularly prevalent in advertisements and sales presentations associated with universal life insurance.

Suppose someone emphasizes that an interest rate of 12 percent will be credited to your cash-value account. What that person may fail to tell you or at least fail to emphasize is that an expense charge of 8 percent will be imposed. In other words, suppose you pay a $1,000 premium. The company will take out an expense charge of $80 (8 percent of $1,000) and credit $920 to your cash-value account. The company will then credit your account with $110 of interest (12 percent of $920), making your account $1,030. If you start the year with $1,000 and end the year with $1,030, you have earned 3 percent interest, not 12 percent. This example, while oversimplified, illustrates the problems associated with the emphasis on gross interest rates rather than net interest rates.

If the interest rates mentioned in the life insurance policy are not indicative of the rate of return on the savings component, and if gross interest rates mentioned in universal life sales illustrations are not indicative of the rate of return on the savings component, what, then, is the rate of return on the savings component? The question—when asked in that fashion—is unanswerable because there is no such figure as *the* rate of return on the savings component of a cash-value life insurance policy.

Suppose you are examining a package called AB. It consists of an item A and an item B. If the price of the package is $100, what is the price of item B? When the question is asked in that fashion, it is unanswerable because there is no such figure as *the* price of item B. You can make a statement about the price of item B only by making an assumption about the price of item A. For example, assume that the price of item A is $30. Then you can say that the price of item B is $70. Note that this figure holds only when you assume that the price of item A is $30.

In the case of cash-value life insurance, the package consists of a protection component and a savings component. To determine a rate of return on the savings component, a price of the protection component must be assumed. In other words, it cannot be said that any one figure is *the* rate of return on the savings component; rather, it can be said that a particular rate of return applies only when a particular price of the protection component is assumed.

Let's take a specific case to illustrate the point. Consider the eighth year of the hypothetical $100,000 straight life policy for which data were shown in Table 3 on page 27. To determine the rate of return on the savings component, it is necessary to make an assumption about the price of the protection component. If it is assumed that the price per $1,000 of protection in the eighth year is $4, the rate of return on the savings component in that year is about 7.1 percent. (The details of this calculation are explained in Appendix E.) If the assumed price of the protection component is reduced, the rate of return on the savings component is reduced; if the assumed price of the protection component is increased, the rate of return on the savings component is increased. For example, various assumed prices per $1,000 of the protection component in the eighth year produce rates of return on the savings component as shown in Table 4.

Table 4
Rates of Return on Savings Component in Eighth Year of Hypothetical Straight Life Policy

Assumed Price per $1,000 of Protection	Rate of Return
$0	3.2%
1	4.2
2	5.2
3	6.2
4	7.1
5	8.1
6	9.1

If a person wants to show that the savings component provides a high rate of return, all that person has to do is assume that the price of the protection component is high. Suppose, for example, that a company charges a high price for one-year renewable term. The agent can use that high price as the price-of-protection assumption in order to calculate the rate of return on the savings component of the company's straight life policy. The result is an apparently high rate of return, but the fact is that the company simply charges a high price for one-year renewable term.

Although there is no such figure as *the* rate of return on the savings component of a cash-value life insurance policy, it is possible to generalize carefully on the subject. If you examine "good" cash-value policies issued by "good" companies, and if you make "reasonable" assumptions concerning the price of the protection component, the rates of return generally will be similar to the rates of return on comparable fixed-dollar savings media. (Procedures for identifying "good" cash-value policies issued by "good" companies are discussed in Chapters 7 and 8.)

More important, however, you should not emphasize rates of return when you are considering life insurance. The primary purpose of life insurance is to provide protection, and for that reason your emphasis should be on the price of the protection component. In order to calculate the price of the protection component, it is necessary to make an assumption about the rate of return on the savings component. In this book, an interest rate of 6 percent generally has been assumed. That figure was selected as representative of what can be earned on various fixed-dollar savings media similar to the savings component of cash-value life insurance policies.

Income Tax Consequences

As a fixed-dollar savings medium, the savings component of a cash-value life insurance policy resembles bank savings accounts, savings and loan accounts, credit union share accounts, and United States savings bonds. In the income tax arena, however, the savings component of cash-value life insurance differs substantially from these other savings media.

By this time it should be evident that interest is important in the structure of a cash-value life insurance policy. Without the interest factor, an insurance company would have to charge much higher premiums to provide for death benefits, cash values, dividends in the case of participating policies, expenses, and profit. As you pay premiums, therefore, interest is at work. Sometimes the interest built into the structure of a cash-value policy is referred to as the "inside interest" or the "inside interest build-up."

To illustrate the income tax treatment of the inside interest, let's assume you buy a $100,000 nonparticipating straight life policy for which the premium is $1,500 per year. Further, let's assume you pay premiums for ten years. During the ten years, inside interest is at work on your behalf, but you do not have to declare any interest as taxable income during that period.

Now let's assume that you discontinue premium payments at the end of the tenth year, and that you receive the cash value. The amount you receive will be equal to, greater than, or less than the total of the premiums you paid.

First, let's assume that the cash value is $15,000, or exactly equal to the total of the ten $1,500 premiums you paid. Under current income tax rules, you have no taxable income. The inside interest is income-tax-deferred until you surrender the policy, and then you are allowed to apply the cost of the protection against the inside interest. In other words, the inside interest for the ten years is equal to the cost of the protection for the ten years. If you buy one-year renewable term and put the difference in premiums into a savings account, the cost of the protection is not deductible, and the interest on the savings account is taxable in the year earned. By acquiring the cash-value policy, you are allowed to apply the cost of the protection against the inside interest.

Second, let's assume that the cash value is $16,000, or exactly $1,000 more than the total of the ten $1,500 premiums you paid. Under current income tax rules, you have taxable income of $1,000. Here again, you are allowed to apply the cost of the protection against the inside interest, and you are taxed only on the amount by which the inside interest exceeds the cost of the protection.

Third, let's assume that the cash value is $14,000, or exactly $1,000 less than the total of the ten $1,500 premiums you paid. In this instance, the cost of the protection exceeds the inside interest by $1,000. Under current income tax rules, you are not allowed a deduction, because the cost of the protection is not deductible, but you are allowed to apply the cost of the protection against the inside interest so as to eliminate any taxable income.

Finally, let's assume that, instead of surrendering the policy at the end of the tenth year, you die at that time. If you own the policy at the time of your death, the $100,000 death benefit of your life insurance is part of your gross estate for federal estate tax purposes. But there is no taxable income to your beneficiary. This is sometimes mentioned as a tax advantage of life insurance, but it is not. Rather, it means that life insurance is treated at death like other property.

For example, suppose you put the $1,500 per year for ten years into common stock. Assume for convenience that no cash dividends are paid and that the stock by the end of ten years grows miraculously to $100,000 in market value. If you own the stock at the time of your death, the stock at its market value of $100,000 is part of your gross estate for federal estate tax purposes. But there is no taxable income or taxable capital gain to your beneficiary. When the stock is subsequently sold, the gain or loss on the transaction is measured from the $100,000 market value of the stock at the time of your death. In other words, the tax treatment of the common stock in this illustration is the same as the tax treatment of the life insurance.

The handling of inside interest from an income tax standpoint constitutes a substantial tax advantage for the savings component of cash-value life insurance, compared with other similar savings media. In the case of bank savings accounts, savings and loan accounts, and credit union share accounts, the interest is taxable income in the year earned. In the case of United States savings bonds, the interest is taxable income when earned or it may be deferred, at the option of the bondholder. But in the case of cash-value life insurance, the inside interest is not only deferred for income tax purposes, but later is either entirely or substantially eliminated. Thus, when a person buys a cash-value life insurance policy, he or she acquires an important income tax shelter. The higher the income tax bracket of the policy-owner, the more important the tax shelter is. This advantage explains why cash-value life insurance often is attractive to persons in high income tax brackets.

Liquidity

The cash value of a life insurance policy is a highly liquid savings medium. It is similar in this respect to bank savings accounts, savings and loan accounts, and credit union share accounts, and is more liquid than United States savings bonds.

There are three ways to obtain access to the savings component of a cash-value life insurance policy. First, the policy can be surrendered for its cash value. This approach, however, means that the protection component of the policy is terminated. For that reason, life insurance cash values would not compare favorably with savings accounts in terms of liquidity if this were the only way in which the policyowner could gain access to the funds.

Second, the policy can be pledged as collateral for a loan. Normally such a transaction is carried out with a commercial bank, but the lender may be some other type of financial institution or even an individual. A loan up to the amount of the cash value usually is regarded as fully secured. This arrangement is made possible through the policy's assignment clause, which is discussed in Chapter 9.

Third, the policyowner can obtain a loan from the life insurance company. Here again the funds available are any amounts up to the cash value. This arrangement is made possible through the policy's loan clause, which is discussed in Chapter 11.

Life insurance cash values are superior to United States savings bonds in terms of liquidity. Savings bonds have no loan clause and are "not transferable," which is another way of saying they cannot be pledged (or "assigned") as collateral for a loan. The only way a bond-holder can obtain access to the funds is to cash in the bond. This is costly, because the effective interest rate when the bond is redeemed prior to maturity is less than the effective interest rate when the bond is held to maturity.

Some critics of life insurance argue that cash values are not as liquid as a savings account because, if you take a policy loan, "you have to pay interest on your own money," while if you take money from a savings account you do not have to pay interest. This argument is without merit, because you lose interest when you draw funds from a savings account. The effect on your financial condition of a with-drawal from a savings account is identical to that of a policy loan in terms of both cost and liquidity, if the interest rate paid on the savings account is equal to the policy loan interest rate.

Suppose you have $10,000 in a savings account earning 6 percent interest. You also have a $100,000 straight life policy with a $10,000 cash value and a 6 percent policy loan interest rate. You decide to buy a $6,000 car.

Suppose you draw the $6,000 from your savings account and then replace the funds at the end of one year (when you receive a bonus from your employer). You lose $360 in interest on your savings account (6 percent of $6,000); so to restore your account fully you have to deposit an additional $360.

But suppose you take a $6,000 policy loan instead of withdrawing the funds from your savings account. Again, you repay the loan at the end of one year, together with $360 interest (6 percent of $6,000). You are now back where you would have been without the loan.

Either way, you take $6,000 in cash to buy the car and pay back $6,360 at the end of one year. Whether you draw the funds from your savings account or take a policy loan, your savings account is now $10,600 (the original $10,000 enhanced by one year's interest), and your cash value is about $11,000 (because the policy is now one year older and an additional annual premium has been paid). Your liquid assets are now $21,600 and your nonliquid asset is a one-year-old car.

In the case of a savings account, the funds normally can be obtained quickly by going to the bank. In the case of a policy loan, if you live near an insurance company office authorized to issue policy loan checks, you can get the funds as quickly as from a bank. In the usual case, however, policy loans are delayed by the need to use the mail and may take about as long as a savings account withdrawal by mail. In short, the loan clause makes the liquidity of the savings component of a cash-value life insurance policy similar to that of a savings account.

Safety

As mentioned earlier, proponents of cash-value life insurance describe cash values as "guaranteed." This expression means that the cash values, and therefore the annual increases in cash values, are backed by the full resources of the life insurance company. In the case of a large, well-established company, these guarantees are significant. Only occasionally does one hear of large life insurance companies in serious financial difficulties.

The guarantees usually can be relied upon even in the case of smaller and younger companies. When a company gets into financial difficulties, it may be taken over by another company. When this happens, the acquiring company carries out the guarantees provided in the policies issued by the defunct company. Companies are willing to absorb another company not only because they want to preserve public confidence in life insurance, but also because a takeover may be a profitable venture.

In addition to the guarantees in the policy, many contracts are participating. In such dividend-paying policies, the financial difficulties of the company may result in smaller dividends for the policyowner than would have been paid in the absence of such difficulties. Policyowner losses of this type may be substantial.

Frequently savings accounts are covered by the Federal Deposit Insurance Corporation, savings and loan accounts by the Federal Savings and Loan Insurance Corporation, and credit union share accounts by the National Credit Union Administration. United States savings bonds are backed by the integrity of the federal government and are considered safe.

Life insurance companies are regulated primarily by the various states rather than by the federal government. Some but not all of the states have guaranty funds or guaranty associations designed to meet the obligations of defunct companies. However, no life insurance guaranty fund is available at the federal level.

The financial integrity of the life insurance company you select, therefore, is important. If you follow the suggestions in Chapter 7, you are not likely to buy insurance from a company that will fail to meet its obligations under the policy.

Forced Savings

People tend to assign a high priority to the payment of life insurance premiums. Since the premiums for cash-value life insurance policies provide for both protection and savings, the result is an element of compulsion that is missing from most other savings media.

The notion of "forced savings" in the context of life insurance might be described better as "semi-compulsion." The policyowner does not have to pay the premiums. Furthermore, the frequent use of the policy loan clause can disrupt a systematic savings program as thoroughly as do frequent withdrawals from a savings account. And today, with the advent of flexible premium life insurance policies (such as universal life), frequent reductions in the premium payments can disrupt a systematic savings program as thoroughly as do frequent withdrawals from a savings account.

Proponents of cash-value life insurance often emphasize the notion of forced savings. They say that people tend to keep their life insurance policies in force, but constantly open and close savings accounts. They suggest that this characteristic of cash-value life insurance is valuable to the policyowner.

Opponents of cash-value life insurance, on the other hand, often express contempt for the notion of forced savings. They say that many policyowners discontinue their policies, and that the use of the forced savings argument by life insurance agents means that the buyer is accused of a lack of self-discipline. They suggest that this characteristic of cash-value life insurance is of little or no value to the policyowner.

The answer, as in many controversial areas, lies between the extreme arguments. Also, the question is a highly subjective and personal one. No one can tell you whether you will be more successful with a systematic savings program in life insurance cash values than with some other savings medium.

Perhaps your experience to date can shed some light on the question. If you have been successful in accumulating savings in other media, the forced savings aspect of cash-value life insurance may be of little value to you. If you have been unsuccessful to date, the semi-compulsion may be of value. In short, the value to you of this characteristic of cash-value life insurance is something you must decide for yourself.

Protection from Creditors

Many of the assets a person owns can be attached by creditors to satisfy a debt. The savings component of a cash-value life insurance policy, however, can be an exception—sometimes it cannot be successfully attached by a creditor.

The importance of this characteristic of cash values is subjective and perhaps impossible to assess. First, many policyowners who get into financial difficulties borrow against their life insurance policies at some time prior to the imposition of strong pressure by their creditors. If such policyowners borrow the maximum under the policy loan clause, no savings component will be left for the creditors to attach.

Second, the question of the availability of cash values to creditors of the policyowner is a complex subject. It is difficult to determine in advance what would happen in any given situation, and no attempt is made here to go into detail. Suffice it to say that the savings component of a cash-value life insurance policy may enjoy an advantage over many other kinds of assets in the event the policyowner gets into financial difficulties.

Life Annuity Rates

The funds provided by a life insurance policy may be paid to the recipient in a single sum or in one of a variety of installment arrangements known as "settlement options," which are discussed in Chapters 9 and 11. Some of the settlement options are life annuities that provide periodic payments to the recipient for as long as he or she lives.

Settlement options are available for funds payable at death under nearly any type of life insurance policy. For cash-value policies, settlement options also are generally available to the policyowner in lieu of a single payment when the policy is discontinued during the insured's lifetime. This means that the savings accumulation in a cash-value policy may be used to produce a life income for the policyowner, or perhaps for both the policyowner and his or her spouse.

The amount of the periodic income provided under a life annuity is determined by calculations similar to those made for life insurance premiums; that is, interest, mortality, expense, and profit assumptions are made. The results of such calculations frequently are shown in the life insurance policy, so that the policyowner is guaranteed a fixed lifetime income for each $1,000 of cash value.

The person who accumulates savings through a cash-value life insurance policy, therefore, obtains what amounts to an upper limit on the prices of a variety of life annuities that may be used many years in the future. If life annuity premium rates increase in the future, the policyowner will have a valuable set of guarantees in the policy. If life annuity premium rates decline, the policyowner can take the cash value in a single sum and purchase a larger life annuity in the open market. Some policies provide an option under which the policyowner is guaranteed the right to purchase a life annuity at a price equal to or slightly below current market rates.

There is at least a possibility of major developments that will extend longevity. The effect of such developments may be increases in life annuity premium rates, and under such circumstances the life annuity settlement options in cash-value life insurance policies may be valuable. It is difficult to put a price tag on the value of the settlement options, but they are worth considering in any examination of the characteristics of the savings component of cash-value life insurance policies.

Chapter 6

How to Select an Appropriate Type of Life Insurance

How the life insurance buyer should select an appropriate type of policy is one of the most hotly debated subjects in the life insurance industry. Some life insurance agents boast they never sell term insurance, and some say term insurance is a ripoff. On the other hand, some life insurance agents boast they never sell cash-value insurance, and some say cash-value insurance is a ripoff.

Once again, the truth lies between the extreme positions. Term insurance and cash-value insurance are two markedly different types of life insurance, and your choice between them should be based upon your financial circumstances and objectives. Once you have determined your life insurance needs, along the lines discussed in Chapter 2, you should decide how much (if any) of those needs you want to meet with straight life. The purpose of this chapter is to help you with that decision. Then the remainder of your needs may be met with one-year renewable term.

The Savings Decision

To decide how much straight life to buy (if any), ask yourself how much you want to invest per year in the savings component of cash-value life insurance. The answer may be reached in three steps. First, decide upon the total amount you want to set aside in savings each year. Second, decide upon the proportion of that total you want to place in fixed-dollar savings media. Third, decide upon the proportion of fixed-dollar savings you want to invest in the savings component of cash-value life insurance.

To make these decisions, it is important for you to understand the nature of the savings component in cash-value life insurance. The characteristics of the savings component are discussed in Chapter 5.

Suppose you decide to invest nothing in the savings component of cash-value life insurance. In that case, you should meet all of your life insurance needs with one-year renewable term. Exercise caution if you follow this route, however. Some of your life insurance needs may continue well beyond the usual retirement age, and for that reason you may want to continue at least a portion of your life insurance protection for a long time. One-year renewable term premiums are high at advanced ages, and the coverage may not be renewable beyond age 65 or 70. Conversion of one-year renewable term (as discussed in Chapter 10) is a possibility, but the premiums for straight life may become prohibitive when conversion is delayed for many years.

Suppose you decide to invest some amount in the savings component of cash-value life insurance each year. The next step, then, is to translate that annual amount of savings into an amount of straight life. Since the savings components of most straight life policies are similar in size, a few representative figures will suffice. Roughly speaking, over a ten-year period, the average yearly amounts that go into the savings component of a straight life policy per $1,000 of death benefit are shown in Table 5.

Table 5
**Average Annual Amounts Added
to Savings Component of Straight
Life Policy**

Age at Issue	Average Annual Amount
20	$ 5.00
25	6.00
30	7.50
35	9.00
40	11.00
45	13.00
50	15.00
55	17.50
60	20.00
65	22.50

The amounts shown in Table 5 were derived in a simple fashion. Each figure represents the sum that would have to be invested at the beginning of each year for ten years, at an interest rate of 6 percent compounded annually, to accumulate an amount that approximates the cash value per $1,000 of death benefit at the end of the tenth year of a typical straight life policy.

To illustrate, suppose you are between 35 and 40 years of age and have decided you need $150,000 of life insurance. Also, suppose you have decided to invest about $500 per year in the savings component of cash-value life insurance. According to Table 5, the average yearly amount that goes into the savings component is about $10 for each $1,000 of death benefit. Under these circumstances, you should buy $50,000 of straight life to invest about $500 per year in the savings component. To meet your total life insurance needs you should then buy the remaining $100,000 in the form of one-year renewable term.

What You Can Afford

If you follow the procedure described in Chapter 2 for estimating your life insurance needs, you may discover that you need more life insurance than you previously thought necessary. Some individuals become discouraged at this point because they assume they will not be able to afford the amount of protection required. Don't be discouraged, however. You may find that life insurance does not cost as much as you thought, and that you are able to buy more protection than you thought you could afford.

Many individuals have the wrong impression about the cost of life insurance protection because they are confused about the distinction between life insurance premiums and the prices of life insurance protection. In the case of cash-value life insurance, the premiums provide not only for life insurance protection but also for a savings component. For that reason, in many of the early policy years, the prices of protection are much smaller than the premiums. In the case of term insurance, if the policy is participating, the dividends make the prices of the protection smaller than the premiums.

At this point you may want to make an estimate of how much it would cost to meet your life insurance needs. The benchmark prices in Table 9 on page 84 can be used to make such an estimate. Multiply the benchmark price for your present age by the number of thousands of death benefit you want to buy. The product is the amount you may expect to pay per year during the early policy years, excluding any front-end load.

To illustrate, suppose you are between 35 and 40 years of age and want to buy $150,000 of life insurance. The benchmark price of $3 for your age, multiplied by 150 (the number of thousands of death benefit), produces $450, which is an estimate of what the life insurance protection will cost you per year during the early policy years, excluding any front-end load.

After you follow this procedure, you may discover that you cannot afford all of the life insurance you need. Under these circumstances, you may want to abandon the idea of using life insurance as a savings medium, and buy as much one-year renewable term as you can afford. Another possibility is to reassess your family's financial requirements in the event of your death, especially if you were generous in determining your life insurance needs initially.

To the extent that you decide to use cash values as a savings medium, you should buy straight life or one of the other cash-value types of life insurance discussed in Chapter 3. To the extent that you decide not to use cash values as a savings medium, you should buy one-year renewable term.

Chapter 7

How to Select a Life Insurance Company

Nearly two thousand life insurance companies exist in the United States today. Some of these are major financial institutions, some are small and may be undercapitalized, and some are between these extremes. Your objective in the selection of a life insurance company should be to buy your life insurance from a company that is financially strong, that offers life insurance at competitive prices, and that issues policies containing provisions favorable to policyowners. This chapter discusses the identity problem, mutual companies versus stock companies, and financial strength. It also contains listings of some suggested companies and an explanation of how the listings were constructed. Subsequent chapters deal with prices and policy provisions.

The Identity Problem

The similarity of company names presents a problem because there are so many companies and so few names that companies are willing to adopt. Popular in the life insurance business are names that suggest financial strength (Guaranty, Protective, Reserve, Security), financial sophistication (Bankers, Commercial, Financial, Investors), maturity (Colonial, First, Old, Pioneer), dependability (Assurance, Great, Reliable, Trust), fair treatment (Beneficial, Equitable, Golden Rule, Progressive), intimacy or friendliness (Citizens, Family, Home, Peoples), breadth of operations (Continental, National, International, Universal), and government (American, Republic, State, United States). Also, many companies are named after well known Americans (Franklin, Jefferson, Lincoln, Washington).

Confusion arises easily and often. For example, an agent of The National Life & Accident Insurance Company (home office: Nashville, TN) wrote a letter to the author of a study that supposedly mentioned the agent's company. The agent had not seen the study, but a prospective customer had told him about it. But the study did not mention his company; rather, his customer had misinterpreted a reference to National Life Insurance Company (home office: Montpelier, VT).

Similarly, considerable confusion is found among Bankers Life Company (home office: Des Moines, IA), Bankers Life Insurance Company of Nebraska (home office: Lincoln, NE), and other companies whose names include the word "Bankers." Bankers of Iowa for several years has been identifying itself in its advertising as "The Bankers Life," a tactic which some might consider a blatant dismissal of the other companies with "Bankers" in their names.

Considerable confusion is also found between The Equitable Life Assurance Society of the United States (New York, NY) and Equitable Life Insurance Company of Iowa (Des Moines, IA); between The Northwestern Mutual Life Insurance Company (Milwaukee, WI) and Northwestern National Life Insurance Company (Minneapolis, MN); and between The Security Mutual Life Insurance Company (Lincoln, NE) and Security Mutual Life Insurance Company of New York (Binghamton, NY).

Confusion also arises because some companies' names are close to mirror images of one another. Two such companies are American United Life Insurance Company (Indianapolis, IN) and United American Insurance Company (Dallas, TX). Two others are Fidelity Union Life Insurance Company (Dallas, TX) and Union Fidelity Life Insurance Company (Trevose, PA).

To illustrate further the proliferation of names, consider some of the companies whose names begin with Lincoln. The Lincoln National Life Insurance Company (Fort Wayne, IN) is a major company. An agent representing "The Lincoln," however, might be representing Lincoln National or one of the following companies:

> Lincoln American Life Insurance Company (Memphis, TN)
> Lincoln Benefit Life Company (Lincoln, NE)
> Lincoln Heritage Life Insurance Company (Phoenix, AZ)
> Lincoln Income Life Insurance Company (Louisville, KY)
> Lincoln Liberty Life Insurance Company (Los Angeles, CA)
> Lincoln Life and Casualty Company (Lincoln, NE)
> Lincoln Mutual Life and Casualty Insurance Company (Fargo, ND)
> Lincoln Mutual Life Insurance Company (Lincoln, NE)
> Lincoln Security Life Insurance Company (Avon, CT)

Some names say something about the companies. For example, Lutheran Brotherhood specializes in selling insurance to Lutherans; Ministers Life—A Mutual Life Insurance Company specializes in selling insurance to individuals in church-related professions; Teachers Insurance and Annuity Association of America specializes in selling insurance and annuities to employees of colleges, universities, and certain other nonprofit educational institutions; and New York Life Insurance Company has its home office in New York City.

On the other hand, some names carry confusing or misleading connotations. For example, The United States Life Insurance Company in the City of New York, often called United States Life, is not an agency of the United States government, is not connected in any way with the United States government, and should not have its life insurance confused with the various forms of subsidized, low-priced life insurance available to United States military personnel and veterans. Chase National Life Insurance Company is not connected with the Chase Manhattan Bank. The Columbus Mutual Life Insurance Company is not a mutual company; it is a stock company owned by The Western and Southern Life Insurance Company. (The distinction between mutual companies and stock companies is discussed later in this chapter.) International Service Life Insurance Company does not operate outside the United States; it is licensed in only twelve states. Mammoth Life and Accident Insurance Company is not a large company; it is a small company with about $28 million in assets as of the end of 1983. Old Western Life Insurance Company is not an old company; it was organized in 1976 and commenced business in 1978.

In view of all the confusion surrounding company names, you should obtain the full name and home office location of any company you are considering. Further, you should assume that the name of the company has no relationship to the nature of the company or its activities.

Mutual Companies versus Stock Companies

Most of the life insurance in the United States is sold by either stock companies or mutual companies. A stock life insurance company is a corporation in which there are stockholders. A mutual life insurance company is a corporation in which there are no stockholders.

Some people say mutual companies offer lower prices to their policyowners because there are no stockholders to share the earnings. Implicit in such a view is the notion that other things are equal—but they never are. Some mutual companies sell high-priced insurance, and some stock companies sell low-priced insurance. Also, although the policyowners of a mutual company technically elect the members of the board of directors, policyowners do not have any effective control over such elections.

Some people say mutual companies are an anachronism in a capitalistic society. Nevertheless, mutual companies pay federal income taxes under the same law as stock companies, and they pay state premium taxes under the same laws as stock companies. Also, some mutual companies pay large salaries to their top officials, and the prospect of even larger salaries provides a profit motive.

Mutual companies usually are associated with participating life insurance (on which dividends are paid to policyowners); however, a few mutual companies also sell nonparticipating insurance. Stock companies usually are associated with nonparticipating life insurance; however, many stock companies also sell participating policies, and a few sell only participating policies. Thus, a decision on whether to buy participating or nonparticipating insurance is different from a decision on whether to buy from a mutual company or a stock company.

Other than the presence or absence of stockholders, differences between these two forms of corporate organization are hard to identify. Do not be concerned about whether a company is mutual or stock. Be concerned only about the company's financial strength, the price of its insurance, and the provisions in its policies.

Financial Strength

Buy your life insurance from a company that is financially strong. With luck it will be a long time between the day you buy life insurance and the day the company is called upon to pay the death benefit. Regardless of the length of that period, however, you want to be sure that the company will be in a financial position to meet its obligations upon your death or when you decide to use the funds in the savings component of a cash-value policy.

Life insurance companies have a good safety record, as mentioned in Chapter 5. However, when companies have financial difficulties, the problems for policyowners can be severe. A recent widely publicized case involved several of the insurance subsidiaries of Baldwin-United Corporation. In this case, owners of annuities received a substantially lower rate of interest than anticipated, and were severely restricted in the extent to which they were allowed access to their funds.

As pointed out in Chapter 5, no federal insurance program is available for life insurance. Although some states have guaranty arrangements under which other life insurance companies are assessed to help meet the obligations of failed companies, you should restrict your dealings to companies that are financially strong in order to minimize the likelihood of delay, red tape, and financial loss.

Your state insurance department is a source of information about life insurance companies. (The addresses of the various state insurance departments are listed in Appendix C.) Unfortunately, you will not be able to find out from your department whether the company is financially strong. The department is not in the business of promoting companies or making derogatory statements about companies. Even if a company is in severe financial distress, the department will not tell you about it unless official action has already been taken. The timing of public dislosure of an insurance company's financial difficulties is a delicate problem for insurance regulators, because disclosure of the difficulties has the effect of aggravating those difficulties and making it harder for the company to recover its financial health.

In some states, requirements for the licensing of an insurance company are rigorous. In other states, the requirements are meager. Since life insurance is a cornerstone of your family's financial affairs, you should require more of a company than simply a license to do business in your state.

The leading firm in the business of analyzing the financial strength of insurance companies is the A. M. Best Company (Oldwick, NJ). Each year two large volumes entitled *Best's Insurance Reports* are published—one covering life insurance companies, and the other covering property-liability insurance companies. These volumes are expensive, but may be found in many libraries.

Best assigns ratings to many of the companies on which it reports. The rating classifications are as follows:

A+ (Excellent)
Contingent A+ (Excellent)
A (Excellent)
Contingent A (Excellent)

B+ (Very Good)
Contingent B+ (Very Good)
B (Good)
Contingent B (Good)

C+ (Fairly Good)
Contingent C+ (Fairly Good)
C (Fair)
Contingent C (Fair)

Omitted
Inapplicable
Deferred
Not Eligible
Not Assigned

In Best's 1984 life edition, 1,600 companies are included. Of these, 268 are rated A+. To be conservative, buy only from a company with an A+ rating from Best. To be more conservative, buy only from a company with ten consecutive years of top ratings in Best's life editions of 1975 through 1984. The 115 companies meeting this test are listed in Appendix B.*

Read Best's report on any company you are considering. When you do so, you should recognize that Best follows the procedure of damning with faint praise. You already may have noted that no companies are rated A−, B−, or C−, and that no companies are rated D or F. Although a report on a company may contain some information on the company's history, a description of its management and operation, and some statistics, unfavorable comments are rare. Usually one finds either favorable comments or no comments. The adjectives and adverbs used must be interpreted carefully.

To illustrate Best's "code," consider the discussion of the quality of a company's investment portfolio. For many companies, the statement is made that "We consider the bond portfolio to be of excellent quality." If it is described as "of very good quality" or "of good quality," or, even worse, if nothing is said about its quality, watch out.

Similarly, consider the discussion of the quality of a company's management. For many companies, the statement is made that the company has been "most ably managed." If the company is described as "very ably managed" or "ably managed," or, even worse, if nothing is said about the quality of the company's management, beware.

Two aspects of the procedure of damning with faint praise should be mentioned. First, Best is an insurance trade publisher. In addition to its reports, it publishes monthly magazines and other items for purchase by the insurance industry. It sells advertising in its magazines to insurance companies and other organizations. It sells abridged reprints of its reports to insurance companies, so that the companies can distribute the reprints to their agents for distribution to policyowners and prospective policyowners. If Best were to publish direct criticism of the companies on which it reports, advertising revenue and reprint sales might be reduced.

Second, Best fears that direct criticism—"calling a spade a spade"— might lead to harassment of the publisher through libel suits by insurance companies that believe they have been criticized unjustly. Furthermore, Best is concerned that direct criticism of an insurance

---

*Prior to its 1976 life edition, Best used a system of recommendations rather than ratings, and used adjectives and adverbs rather than letters. The companies listed in Appendix B received the most-strongly worded recommendation in the life edition of 1975, and A+ ratings in the life editions of 1976 through 1984.

company in trouble might magnify the difficulty and even destroy the company, which might otherwise overcome the difficulty. These thoughts may be justified or they may be mere rationalizations of Best's policies. In any case, be aware that Best's reporting system results in subtle hints rather than clearly stated information for buyers.

The technical details of the procedure by which Best decides upon its ratings and upon the various adjectives and adverbs have not been published and are not made available for scrutiny by outsiders. Nevertheless, the nature of its reports shows that Best engages in astute financial analysis of insurance companies, and it is a respected publishing firm. You should use its ratings, because nothing better exists for evaluating the financial strength of insurance companies.

It is extremely important that you avoid reliance on organizations that imitate the A. M. Best Company. For example, an organization called "Dunne's" (not to be confused with Dun & Bradstreet) for many years gave A+ ratings to companies with lower Best ratings. And an organization called "Standard Analytical Service" prepares brief reports containing highly favorable comments about many companies that receive ratings below A+ from Best.

Suggested Companies

Two separate listings of suggested companies for buyers of life insurance—one listing for buyers of one-year renewable term and another for buyers of cash-value insurance—were published during 1983 in *The Insurance Forum.** The listings were based on separate surveys. In each instance, companies with ten consecutive years of top ratings by the A. M. Best Company were asked to participate in the study. About half the companies participated. The prices and policy provisions of the responding companies were examined. These topics are discussed in the next four chapters.

For one-year renewable term, the companies listed are those offering competitively priced policies containing provisions favorable to policyowners. For cash-value life insurance, the companies listed are those offering competitively priced policies to new policyowners, providing competitively priced coverage currently to existing policyown-

---

*The Insurance Forum is a four-page monthly periodical. Its editor is the author of this book.

ers, and issuing policies containing provisions favorable to policy-owners.

The suggested companies for buyers of one-year renewable term are shown in Table 6. The suggested companies for buyers of cash-value insurance are shown in Table 7. In both cases you should follow the procedures described in this book for the selection of a policy even if you are considering the purchase of a policy from one of the suggested companies.

Table 6
Suggested Companies for Buyers of One-Year Renewable Term
Life Insurance
(listed alphabetically)

Company	Home Office
Bankers Life Company	Des Moines, IA
Central Life Assurance Company	Des Moines, IA
Connecticut Mutual Life Insurance Company	Hartford, CT
General American Life Insurance Company	St. Louis, MO
Life Insurance Company of Georgia	Atlanta, GA
Massachusetts Mutual Life Insurance Company	Springfield, MA
Metropolitan Life Insurance Company	New York, NY
Mutual Benefit Life Insurance Company	Newark, NJ
Mutual Trust Life Insurance Company	Oak Brook, IL
National Guardian Life Insurance Company	Madison, WI
National Life Insurance Company	Montpelier, VT
New England Mutual Life Insurance Company	Boston, MA
Northwestern Mutual Life Insurance Company	Milwaukee, WI

Table 7

Suggested Companies for Buyers of Cash-Value Life Insurance (listed alphabetically)

Company	Home Office
Bankers Life Company	Des Moines, IA
Central Life Assurance Company	Des Moines, IA
Connecticut Mutual Life Insurance Company	Hartford, CT
Country Life Insurance Company	Bloomington, IL
Equitable Life Assurance Society of the United States	New York, NY
General American Life Insurance Company	St. Louis, MO
Guardian Life Insurance Company of America	New York, NY
Indianapolis Life Insurance Company	Indianapolis, IN
Lutheran Mutual Life Insurance Company	Waverly, IA
Massachusetts Mutual Life Insurance Company	Springfield, MA
National Guardian Life Insurance Company	Madison, WI
Northwestern Mutual Life Insurance Company	Milwaukee, WI
Phoenix Mutual Life Insurance Company	Hartford, CT
Provident Mutual Life Insurance Company	Philadelphia, PA
Southern Farm Bureau Life Insurance Company	Jackson, MS
Standard Insurance Company	Portland, OR
Teachers Insurance and Annuity Association of America	New York, NY

Chapter 8

The Price of Life Insurance

It is often said that you get what you pay for. The implication is that you get a better product or service if you pay a higher price. In life insurance, perhaps the phrase should read, "the lower the price you pay, the better off you are likely to be." Large price differences are found among life insurance companies for essentially the same coverage, despite what you may have heard to the contrary.

How can these large price differences exist among life insurance companies? Such differences can be found because the companies are successful in their attempt to obscure the price of life insurance. Life insurance buyers and policyowners generally are unaware of the price they pay for life insurance protection, because the vital information is systematically withheld from them. Even companies that generally charge low prices are reluctant to disclose vital information, because price obscurity is an important ingredient in many techniques for selling life insurance.

The purpose of this chapter is to arm you with a procedure for measuring the price of life insurance. Using the procedure requires persistence and effort, but following the procedure is important if you want competitively priced life insurance.

Available Price Information

Throughout the history of life insurance in the United States—until the 1970s—the only price information generally available was based on the so-called traditional net-cost method. Under this method, certain price figures are calculated for various periods of time—often twenty years—without recognition of the time value of money. The resulting figures not only understate the price of life insurance, but also distort comparisons among policies issued by different companies. Furthermore, the widespread use of the traditional net-cost method led to various forms of manipulation, through which policies are designed to appear more favorably priced than they really are.

In the 1970s, the life insurance industry began using the so-called interest-adjusted method. This is the same as the traditional net-cost method, except that the time value of money is recognized. When you buy life insurance today, the chances are good that you will be given some price figures based upon the interest-adjusted method. Unfortunately, the interest-adjusted method is also susceptible to manipulation. And interest-adjusted price figures do not provide you with vital information about a policy's price structure.

You should disregard price information given to you when you buy life insurance. Some of it may be inaccurate, some of it may be deceptive, and none of it is likely to tell you what you need to know. Instead, follow the procedure described in the remainder of this chapter to determine whether the life insurance you are considering is competitively priced.

Gathering Information

It is impractical to search for the lowest possible price; there are too many complications associated with such a search. Furthermore, direct price comparisons of policies issued by different companies are often fraught with difficulties because of important elements of noncomparability. Your objective—simply stated—is to buy life insurance that is competitively priced. To do so, follow these three steps: (1) gather raw data about each policy you want to evaluate, (2) perform calculations using the data gathered in the first step, and (3) compare the results of your calculations with benchmark prices.

You should obtain the following raw data about each policy you are considering:

- the annual premium payable at the beginning of each year
- the cash value (if any) payable on surrender at the end of each year
- the annual dividend (if any) payable at the end of each year, based on the company's current dividend scale
- the death benefit payable at the end of each year

To obtain this information, ask the insurance company or your agent to furnish it to you. A sample letter to the company is shown in Figure 5. Pattern your request after the sample letter, and enclose with your letter a form such as shown in Figure 6.*

Obtain the information for each year through and including at least the year in which you are aged 74. If the company fails to write the information on the form you provided, write the information on the form yourself. If the company fails to provide the information you requested, file a complaint with your state insurance department. The procedure for filing a complaint is described in Chapter 15.

The first seven columns in the form are the same as those in Table 3 on page 27. The first column is the year; it should be numbered consecutively, starting with 1 and ending with the last year for which you have obtained information. The second column should be numbered consecutively, starting with your present age. The third, fourth, fifth, and sixth columns are the four items of raw data mentioned earlier.

Making the Calculations

The seventh column is the amount of protection; it is calculated by subtracting the cash value (column 4) from the death benefit (column

---

*Permission is hereby granted to photocopy the form in Figure 6. Also, an 8½ × 11 reprint of the form is available. Send a stamped, addressed envelope to the author at P. O. Box 245, Ellettsville, IN 47429, and request the data form for a proposed policy.

Figure 5
Sample Letter Requesting Information about a Proposed New Policy

---

1234 North Main Street
Bloomington, IN 47401
June 1, 1985

Mr. Steven S. Smith, President
ABC Life Insurance Company
5678 South Elm Street
Philadelphia, PA 19101

Dear Mr. Smith:

I may buy a $100,000 participating straight life policy from your company. I am now 35. To evaluate the policy, I need the following information for each year through and including at least the year in which I am 74:

1. The annual premium payable at the beginning of each year. Please exclude the premiums for any riders.

2. The cash value (if any) payable on surrender at the end of each year, including any excess interest credited to the cash value based on your current interest rate. Please exclude the effect of any dividends.

3. The annual dividend (if any) payable at the end of each year, based on your current dividend scale. Please exclude the dividends attributable to any riders. Please also exclude any dividends attributable to dividend additions and any interest credited to dividend accumulations.

4. The death benefit payable at the end of each year. Please exclude the death benefit of any riders. Please also exclude the effect of any dividends.

It would be helpful if you would provide the requested information on the enclosed form. If you provide a computer printout, please indicate which figures belong in columns 3 through 6 of the enclosed form. Thank you for providing the information that I have requested.

Sincerely yours,

John J. Jones

Enclosure

---

6). (The reason the amount of protection is the difference between the death benefit and the cash value is explained in Chapter 3.)

The eighth column is the yearly price per $1,000 of protection; it is calculated by using the following formula:

$$YPT = \frac{(P + CVP)(1 + i) - (CV + D)}{(DB - CV)(.001)}$$

where YPT is the yearly price per $1,000 of protection, P is the annual premium, CVP is the cash value at the end of the preceding year,

Figure 6
Form for Recording Information about a Proposed New Policy

Name of company_____

Type of policy _____

(1) Year	(2) Age	(3) Annual Premium	(4) Cash Value	(5) Annual Dividend*	(6) Death Benefit	(7) Amount of Protection**	(8) Yearly Price***	(9) Benchmark Price
1								
2								
3								
4								
5								
6								
7								
8								
9								
10								
11								
12								
13								
14								
15								
16								
17								
18								
19								
20								
21								
22								
23								
24								
25								

(1) Year	(2) Age	(3) Annual Premium	(4) Cash Value	(5) Annual Dividend*	(6) Death Benefit	(7) Amount of Protection**	(8) Yearly Price***	(9) Benchmark Price
26								
27								
28								
29								
30								
31								
32								
33								
34								
35								
36								
37								
38								
39								
40								
41								
42								
43								
44								
45								
46								
47								
48								
49								
50								

*Neither estimates nor guarantees, but merely illustrations of the company's current dividend scale.

**Death benefit (column 6) minus cash value (column 4).

***Yearly price per $1,000 of protection, assuming 6 percent interest.

i is the assumed interest rate expressed as a decimal, CV is the cash value at the end of the year, D is the annual dividend, and DB is the death benefit. (The formula is explained in Appendix D.) Assume an interest rate (i) of 6 percent (.06) in your calculations. (For a discussion of the choice of the assumed interest rate, see Appendix D.)

To illustrate, consider the hypothetical policy for which figures are shown in Table 8. The raw data (columns 3, 4, 5, and 6) for the eighth year of the policy are as follows:

> Annual premium (P): $1,500
> Cash value at end of year (CV): $9,200
> Cash value at end of preceding year (CVP): $7,800
> Annual dividend (D): $400
> Death benefit (DB): $100,000

Your next step is to calculate the yearly price per $1,000 of protection (column 8) for the eighth year by plugging the above figures into the formula. The calculations are as follows:

$$
\begin{aligned}
\text{YPT} &= \frac{(1{,}500 \ + \ 7{,}800)(1 \ + \ .06) \ - \ (9{,}200 \ + \ 400)}{(100{,}000 \ - \ 9{,}200)(.001)} \\[2mm]
&= \frac{(9{,}300)(1.06) \ - \ 9{,}600}{(90{,}800)(.001)} \\[2mm]
&= \frac{9{,}858 \ - \ 9{,}600}{90.8} = \frac{258}{90.8} = 2.84
\end{aligned}
$$

Comparing the Results

The next step is to write the benchmark prices in the ninth column. These are shown in Table 9, and correspond to the age figures you wrote in the second column.

Finally, compare the yearly prices in the eighth column with the benchmarks in the ninth column. The suggested interpretations of the comparisons are as follows:

● To the extent that the yearly prices in the policy you are considering are less than the benchmarks, the prices of the protection are low.

Table 8
Yearly Raw Data and Price Information for Hypothetical $100,000 Partici-pating Straight Life Policy Issued to a Man Aged 35

(1) Year	(2) Age	(3) Annual Premium	(4) Cash Value	(5) Annual Dividend*	(6) Death Benefit	(7) Amount of Protection**	(8) Yearly Price***	(9) Benchmark Price
1	35	$1,500	$ 0	$ 50	$100,000	$100,000	$15.40	$ 3.00
2	36	1,500	1,250	100	100,000	98,750	2.43	3.00
3	37	1,500	2,500	150	100,000	97,500	2.72	3.00
4	38	1,500	3,750	200	100,000	96,250	3.01	3.00
5	39	1,500	5,000	250	100,000	95,000	3.32	3.00
6	40	1,500	6,400	300	100,000	93,600	2.03	4.00
7	41	1,500	7,800	350	100,000	92,200	2.43	4.00
8	42	1,500	9,200	400	100,000	90,800	2.84	4.00
9	43	1,500	10,600	450	100,000	89,400	3.27	4.00
10	44	1,500	12,000	500	100,000	88,000	3.70	4.00
11	45	1,500	13,600	550	100,000	86,400	1.85	6.50
12	46	1,500	15,200	600	100,000	84,800	2.43	6.50
13	47	1,500	16,800	650	100,000	83,200	3.03	6.50
14	48	1,500	18,400	700	100,000	81,600	3.65	6.50
15	49	1,500	20,000	750	100,000	80,000	4.30	6.50
16	50	1,500	21,600	800	100,000	78,400	4.97	10.00
17	51	1,500	23,200	850	100,000	76,800	5.68	10.00
18	52	1,500	24,800	900	100,000	75,200	6.41	10.00
19	53	1,500	26,400	950	100,000	73,600	7.17	10.00
20	54	1,500	28,000	1,000	100,000	72,000	7.97	10.00
21	55	1,500	29,600	1,050	100,000	70,400	8.81	15.00
22	56	1,500	31,200	1,100	100,000	68,800	9.68	15.00
23	57	1,500	32,800	1,150	100,000	67,200	10.60	15.00
24	58	1,500	34,400	1,200	100,000	65,600	11.55	15.00
25	59	1,500	36,000	1,250	100,000	64,000	12.56	15.00
26	60	1,500	37,600	1,300	100,000	62,400	13.62	25.00
27	61	1,500	39,200	1,350	100,000	60,800	14.74	25.00
28	62	1,500	40,800	1,400	100,000	59,200	15.91	25.00
29	63	1,500	42,400	1,450	100,000	57,600	17.15	25.00
30	64	1,500	44,000	1,500	100,000	56,000	18.46	25.00
31	65	1,500	45,600	1,550	100,000	54,400	19.85	35.00
32	66	1,500	47,200	1,600	100,000	52,800	21.33	35.00
33	67	1,500	48,800	1,650	100,000	51,200	22.89	35.00
34	68	1,500	50,400	1,700	100,000	49,600	24.56	35.00
35	69	1,500	52,000	1,750	100,000	48,000	26.33	35.00
36	70	1,500	53,600	1,800	100,000	46,400	28.23	50.00
37	71	1,500	55,200	1,850	100,000	44,800	30.27	50.00
38	72	1,500	56,800	1,900	100,000	43,200	32.45	50.00
39	73	1,500	58,400	1,950	100,000	41,600	34.81	50.00
40	74	1,500	60,000	2,000	100,000	40,000	37.35	50.00

*Neither estimates nor guarantees, but merely illustrations of the company's current dividend scale.
**Death benefit (column 6) minus cash value (column 4).
***Yearly price per $1,000 of protection, assuming 6 percent interest.

- To the extent that the yearly prices in the policy you are considering are more than the benchmarks but less than double the benchmarks, the prices of the protection are moderate.
- To the extent that the yearly prices in the policy you are considering are more than double the benchmarks, the prices of the protection are high.

Table 9
Benchmark Prices and Front-End-Load Multiples

Age	Benchmark Price	Front-End-Load Multiple
Under 30	$ 1.50	10
30–34	2.00	9
35–39	3.00	8
40–44	4.00	7
45–49	6.50	6
50–54	10.00	5
55–59	15.00	4
60–64	25.00	3
65–69	35.00	3
70–74	50.00	3
75–79	80.00	2
80–84	125.00	2

Sources: The benchmark prices were derived from certain United States population death rates, and were first published in the June 1982 issue of *The Insurance Forum.* The benchmark figure for each five-year age bracket is close to the death rate per 1,000 at the highest age in that bracket. The front-end-load multiples were developed by the author from review of the front-end loads in various cash-value policies, and were first published in the June 1984 issue of *The Insurance Forum.*

You should prefer a policy in which the yearly prices are low. In the hypothetical policy in Table 8, for example, the yearly prices are consistently below the benchmarks. The prices of the protection in the hypothetical policy, therefore, are low. The only exception is in the first year, which is discussed in the following section.

The Front-End Load

As a general rule, cash-value life insurance policies are "front-end-loaded"—that is, the prices in the first one or two years are relatively high in order to cover the sales and administrative expenses associated with the issuance of a new policy. Therefore, you may expect to find the prices in the first one or two years to be more than double the benchmarks.

To evaluate the size of the front-end load, refer to the "front-end-load multiples" in Table 9. If the front-end load in the policy you are considering is less than the indicated multiple of the benchmark, the front-end load is small. If the front-end load is more than the multiple but less than double the multiple, the front-end load is medium. If the front-end load is more than double the multiple, the front-end load is large. When considering the size of the front-end load, combine the multiples for the first two years. For example, if the price in the first year is 7 times the benchmark, and if the price in the second year is 5 times the benchmark, the multiple for such a policy is 12.

You should prefer a policy in which the front-end load is small. In the hypothetical policy shown in Table 8, for example, the price in the first year is about 5 times the benchmark, and the price in the second year is about 1 times the benchmark. The sum of the multiples for the two years—6 times the benchmark—is less than the multiple of 8 for age 35, so the front-end load in the hypothetical policy is small.

Guaranteed versus Nonguaranteed Figures

You must understand the distinction between figures that are guaranteed by the insurance company and figures that are not guaranteed. The latter frequently are referred to as "illustrations," because they show what will happen if the insurance company makes no changes in future years in how it arrives at various dollar amounts. The problem is that the insurance company has the right to make changes—substantial changes—that produce results different from those illustrated at the time of sale. The differences between the illustrations and the results may or may not be in your favor; you cannot know in advance either the magnitude or the direction of such differences.

Annual Premiums

In most traditional life insurance policies, the annual premiums are guaranteed. In some traditional policies, however, the annual premiums shown to you at the time of sale are illustrations that are not guaranteed; such cases usually include a schedule of maximum premiums. For example, a company may say that the maximum annual premium is $500, but that the current annual premium is $400. Base your purchase decision on results using the illustrated premiums, but be aware that the results are not guaranteed.

In some policies, such as universal life, the annual premiums are flexible. You can increase or decrease them (within limits) from time to time. The sales illustrations for these policies frequently assume that you will pay premiums in accordance with some schedule, and you should understand that the results shown are based on that assumption.

Cash Values

One-year renewable term policies include no cash values. In traditional cash-value policies, the cash values are guaranteed.

In universal life policies, the cash values shown in sales proposals are based on illustrated (nonguaranteed) interest rates and on illustrated (nonguaranteed) mortality charges. If you are considering the purchase of universal life, base your purchase decision on results using the illustrated figures. However, you should follow the procedure described later in this chapter to determine whether the charges built into the policy are reasonable.

In variable life policies, the cash values are not guaranteed; rather, they are based on the investment results of the securities in the company's variable life account. If you are considering the purchase of variable life, follow the procedure described later in this chapter to determine whether the charges built into the policy are reasonable.

Annual Dividends

For traditional, participating life insurance policies, sales proposals are based upon illustrated (nonguaranteed) annual dividends. While you should base your purchase decision on results using the illustrated dividends, be aware that the results are not guaranteed.

In universal life policies, usually no dividends are shown. Instead, the effect of illustrated (nonguaranteed) interest rates is built into the cash values.

In variable life policies, usually no dividends are shown. Instead, the cash values reflect the investment results of the securities in the company's variable life account.

Death Benefits

In a traditional life insurance policy, the death benefit is guaranteed. In many sales proposals, however, the death benefit is augmented by dividends, on the assumption that you will leave dividends with the company. To determine whether the life insurance you are considering is competitively priced, follow the procedure outlined in this chapter. Under that procedure, it is assumed that you receive each dividend in cash rather than leave it with the company. You may choose to leave dividends with the company, but that choice should be made after the basic purchase decision has been made.

In a universal life policy, the death benefit may be expressed in either of two ways. First, you may purchase a policy in which the death benefit in any year is the sum of a specified figure and the cash value for that year. Since the cash values are based on illustrated (nonguaranteed) interest rates, the death benefit under these circumstances also is not guaranteed. You should base your purchase decision on the results using the illustrated figures, but be aware that the results are not guaranteed.

Second, you may purchase a universal life policy in which the death benefit is specified but includes any cash value that has accumulated. When the policy is in this form, the death benefit is guaranteed.

In a variable life policy, the death benefit is based on the investment results of the securities in the company's variable life account, but usually some minimum death benefit is guaranteed. If you are considering the purchase of variable life, be aware of the speculative quality of the death benefit.

Universal Life

The rate of interest credited to the cash value of a universal life policy is determined by the company from time to time, subject to a minimum interest rate specified in the policy. The marketing of universal life is characterized by heavy emphasis on what appear to be high rates of interest. It is not unusual, for example, to see prominent references to interest rates of 11, 12, or 13 percent in advertisements and sales presentations.

These rates are suspect, for at least two reasons. First, they are gross interest rates that do not reflect any portion of the expense charges built into the policy.

Second, those attractive interest rates will not necessarily be paid. They are not guaranteed, and they may fluctuate sharply with changes in market interest rates. Furthermore, there is no guarantee that in any given future year the insurance company will use for longtime policyowners the same gross interest rate used in sales illustrations shown to prospective buyers in that year. Sales illustrations projecting attractive interest rates many years into the future should be viewed with skepticism.

If you are considering the purchase of universal life, you should follow the procedure described earlier in this chapter, with three modifications. First, when you gather raw data for the policy you are considering, note what gross interest rate was used to generate the cash values and the death benefits. Second, when you calculate yearly prices per $1,000 of protection, assume an interest rate equal to the gross interest rate used to generate the cash values and the death benefits. Third, when you compare the yearly prices with the benchmarks, the suggested interpretations are as follows:

- To the extent that the yearly prices are less than the benchmarks, the combined mortality and expense charges are small.
- To the extent that the yearly prices are more than the benchmarks but less than double the benchmarks, the combined mortality and expense charges are medium.
- To the extent that the yearly prices are more than double the benchmarks, the combined mortality and expense charges are large.

The procedure described above can be used to evaluate the combined mortality and expense charges. However, the procedure will not help you determine what gross interest rates are likely to be paid by the company in the future. For that reason, do not use the procedure to choose among policies issued by various companies. For example, do not use the procedure to choose between two policies whose charges are small. Such a choice should be based on other considerations, such as policy provisions.

Variable Life

If you are considering the purchase of variable life, you may evaluate the policy using the same procedure described above for universal life. In the variable life prospectus, you will find illustrations of cash values and death benefits based upon several hypothetical gross annual rates of investment return. Unfortunately, the prospectus is likely to show figures only for years 1 through 10, and then a few selected later years. These figures are not sufficient. Obtain figures from the company or from your agent for each year through and including at least the year in which you are aged 74.

Sometimes the hypothetical gross annual rates of investment return are 0 percent, 4 percent, and 8 percent, and sometimes the rates are 0 percent, 6 percent, and 12 percent. Select one of the rates and write the raw data on a form such as that shown in Figure 6.

When you calculate yearly prices per $1,000 of protection, assume an interest rate equal to the hypothetical gross annual rate of investment return you selected. For example, if you wrote down the cash values and the death benefits based on a gross annual rate of investment return of 6 percent, assume an interest rate of 6 percent in your price calculations. Then compare the yearly prices with the benchmarks in the manner described earlier for universal life.

Again, this procedure can be used to evaluate the combined mortality and expense charges. However, the procedure will not help you determine what gross annual rate of investment return is likely to be earned by the company. For that reason, do not use the procedure to choose among policies issued by various companies.

Rates of Return

The primary purpose of life insurance is to provide death protection. Therefore, the primary method for evaluating a life insurance policy is to measure the price of the protection, in the manner described earlier in this chapter.

If the policy you are considering contains a savings component, however, you may want to measure the rate of return on the savings component. Yearly rates of return may be calculated using the raw data referred to earlier in this chapter.

To illustrate, consider the eighth year of the hypothetical policy for which data are shown in Table 8. To perform the rate-of-return calculations, you must assume a yearly price per $1,000 of protection (YPT). Use the benchmark price in Table 9 corresponding to your age. Since you are 42 at the beginning of the eighth year of the hypothetical policy, the benchmark price is $4.

Now you are ready to perform the necessary calculations to arrive at a yearly rate of return on the savings component for the eighth year of the hypothetical policy. The formula is as follows:

$$i = \frac{(CV + D) + (YPT)(DB - CV)(.001)}{(P + CVP)} - 1$$

where i is the yearly rate of return on the savings component expressed as a decimal, YPT is the assumed yearly price per $1,000 of
protection, and the other items are the same as in the formula shown
earlier in this chapter for the yearly price per $1,000 of protection.
(The formula is explained in Appendix E.)

Your next step is to plug into the formula the raw data for the
eighth year. The calculations are as follows:

$$i = \frac{(9,200 + 400) + (4)(100,000 - 9,200)(.001)}{(1,500 + 7,800)} - 1$$

$$= \frac{(9,600) + (4)(90,800)(.001)}{(9,300)} - 1$$

$$= \frac{9,600 + 363}{9,300} - 1$$

$$= \frac{9,963}{9,300} - 1 = 1.071 - 1 = .071 = 7.1\%$$

Note that the formula produces a rate of return expressed as a
decimal (.071), which may be converted to a percentage by moving
the decimal point two places to the right. Stated verbally, the yearly
rate of return on the savings component in the eighth year of the
hypothetical policy is 7.1 percent, assuming $4 is the yearly price per
$1,000 of protection. Similar calculations may be performed for the
other years for which you have obtained raw data.

When you evaluate the yearly rate of return on the savings component of the policy you are considering, bear in mind that most
savings vehicles other than the savings component of cash-value life
insurance produce interest income that is subject to current income
tax. The interest earnings built into cash-value life insurance, on the
other hand, are income-tax-deferred and eventually will be either
fully or partially income-tax-exempt. The suggested interpretations
of the results of your rate-of-return calculations are as follows:

- To the extent that the yearly rates of return on the savings component of the policy you are considering are in the vicinity of 6
  percent or more, the rates of return are good.
- To the extent that the yearly rates of return on the savings com-

ponent of the policy you are considering are in the vicinity of 5 percent, the rates of return are fair.

- To the extent that the yearly rates of return on the savings component of the policy you are considering are in the vicinity of 4 percent or less, the rates of return are poor.

To illustrate, the yearly rate of return that came out of your calculations is 7.1 percent. Since that figure is in excess of 6 percent, the rate of return on the savings component at least in the eighth year of the hypothetical policy is good.

The procedure described here for calculating yearly rates of return is a mirror image of the procedure described earlier in this chapter for calculating yearly prices per $1,000 of protection. A low-priced policy will provide a good rate of return on the savings component, and a high-priced policy will provide a poor rate of return on the savings component. In other words, either formula will lead to the same conclusion about whether a policy is favorable or unfavorable from your point of view.

If the cash value of the policy you are considering is zero, the policy has no savings component. This situation occurs not only in most term policies, but also in the first one or two years of many cash-value policies. Under these circumstances, you should disregard yearly rates of return.

If the cash value of the policy you are considering is small (less than, say, 5 percent of the death benefit), the policy has a small savings component. This situation occurs in the early years of many cash-value policies. Under these circumstances, you should disregard yearly rates of return.

Existing Policies

Life insurance companies want to help their agents sell new policies, so the companies have a strong incentive to make their new policies appear attractively priced. In most instances, however, the attractiveness is based primarily upon nonguaranteed illustrations. You never can be sure about the extent to which the illustrated figures will materialize. For that reason, you should find out how the company you are considering treats its longtime policyowners. After all, if you buy a new policy and pay premiums for a number of years, you yourself will become a longtime policyowner of the company.

Chapter 16 describes a procedure for evaluating an existing life insurance policy. To find out how the company you are considering treats its longtime policyowners, assume that you bought a policy from the company many years ago. Then apply the procedure to that policy. For example, assume that you bought a $10,000 policy from the company 25 years ago at the age of 35.

One warning: To avoid being deceived by figures for a policy that the company did not sell extensively, you should select for review a policy that was heavily sold by the company at the time. You may find out whether the policy was heavily sold by asking what percentage of the company's business at the time was represented by the policy you are reviewing.

Chapter 9

Life Insurance Contract Provisions

The life insurance policy is a complex legal document. No attempt is made here to present a thorough analysis of the contract; rather, the purpose of this and the two following chapters is to point out some of the more important aspects that the buyer should understand. Most of the points discussed are unlikely to come up in the typical sales interview unless you initiate the subject.

This chapter contains discussions of contract provisions that are found in life insurance policies generally. Chapter 10 contains discussions of contract provisions that are found in one-year renewable term policies. Chapter 11 contains discussions of contract provisions that are found in cash-value policies such as straight life.

Insuring Agreement

The insuring agreement spells out the basic promise made by the insurance company, although usually it is not possible to understand the nature of the promise without looking at several other provisions of the contract. Here is a sample of the insuring agreement in a life insurance policy:

> The XYZ Life Insurance Company promises to pay the face amount to the beneficiary upon receipt at our home office of due proof of death of the insured, subject to the terms and conditions of this policy. All benefits will be payable subject to the policy provisions.

Brief Description

A brief description of the policy usually is found at the bottom of the first page. It is sometimes helpful to look at the description as a first step toward understanding the nature of the policy, although the description frequently uses words that are a part of the jargon of the life insurance business. Here is how the brief description might read:

> Whole life policy. Participating. Insurance payable at death. Premiums payable for life unless previously paid up by dividends.

Death Benefit

The death benefit is the amount payable upon the death of the person whose life is insured. An important question is whether the company pays interest on the death benefit between the date of death and the date of the settlement check. Some policies provide for interest on the funds for that period, but they also state that the period may not exceed, say, one year.

Some policies, on the other hand, are silent on this point. This means that the company would not be obligated to pay interest from the date of death, although it might do so as a matter of company practice. Be sure to check on this point. If the company does not pay such interest routinely, it may be possible to arrange payments under a settlement option (to be discussed later) so that interest will accrue from the date of death. This item is not small. If the death benefit is

$100,000, the applicable interest rate is 6 percent, and the company does not pay interest from the date of death to the date of the check, the interest loss to your beneficiary will be more than $16 for each day of delay. So if your beneficiary—distraught by your death—were to procrastinate for several weeks in filing the death claim, the loss could amount to hundreds of dollars. Here is how the provision might read:

> If the death benefit is paid in one sum, we will add interest from the date of death to the date of payment. If the death benefit is applied under a settlement option, interest will be paid from the date of death to the effective date of that option.

Another important question is whether the company pays to the beneficiary the unearned portion of the premium. Suppose the policyowner pays a $1,200 annual premium on the due date and then dies three months later. Under such circumstances, many companies pay, in addition to the basic death benefit of the policy, the unearned portion of the premium. In this example, one-fourth of the annual premium is considered "earned" because one-fourth of the year has elapsed between the payment of the premium and the death of the insured. Thus, three-fourths of the premium ($900 in this case) is considered "unearned" and would be paid to the beneficiary in addition to the basic death benefit.

Some companies, on the other hand, consider the premium fully earned when paid. These companies argue that payment of the unearned portion of the premium is additional life insurance, which can be provided only at a cost. Such an argument is correct. Even so, many companies pay the extra amount. Be sure the policy you are considering provides for a refund at death of the unearned portion of any premium previously paid. Here is how the provision might read:

> We will refund, as part of the policy proceeds, that portion of the current premium paid for a period beyond the policy month in which the insured dies.

At this point you may consider that undue emphasis has been placed on a couple of minor points. That may be true, but these two points are evidence of the quality of the contract and of the company from the buyer's point of view. Ironically, you are likely to find these and other favorable provisions in policies that are relatively low-priced. This observation shows one way life insurance contradicts the saying that you get what you pay for.

Beneficiary

The beneficiary clause is an important part of the life insurance contract. It identifies the individual (individuals) or entity (entities) to receive the funds upon the death of the insured.

One alleged advantage of the life insurance contract is the relative ease with which a beneficiary may be designated. It is simple, when compared with the formalities that surround the preparation of a will. Unfortunately, its simplicity leads to carelessness in the designation of beneficiaries.

Consider, for example, the case of Don Taylor, who has a wife and several young children. After a long session with an agent, Don signs up for $100,000 of life insurance. With both Don and his agent getting tired, they quickly dispose of the beneficiary question by using the following common arrangement: "Jill Taylor, wife of the insured, if living; otherwise, their children equally."

The word "children" is not as simple as it looks. In addition to natural children, there may be stepchildren, adopted children, foster children, and illegitimate children; considerable care may be needed to avoid confusion and misunderstanding. Additional children may be born, adopted, or taken in by the family after the insurance is purchased; such events may necessitate changes in the beneficiary designation, but changes are frequently neglected.

Even where the identity of the beneficiaries is not a problem, beneficiary designations can create undesired results. Suppose one of the Taylor children turns out to be a lazy, shiftless bum who likes to spend money on souped-up cars. Another turns out to be a conscientious student who wants to attend law school. And a third develops a serious medical problem that will require substantial sums of money. If both Don and Jill were dead, it might be inappropriate for the three children to share the life insurance funds equally.

One way to handle this type of situation is to have the funds payable to Jill, if living, but otherwise to a trustee (normally the trust department of a commercial bank). Then, through the terms of their wills and a trust agreement drafted by their attorney, the trustee can be given discretion in the use of the funds.

The trust arrangement frequently is appropriate because it is one way to achieve flexibility and discretion concerning the funds. These characteristics are important when young children are the beneficiaries, because the parents do not know what the future holds. When they establish a trust, they hope the trustee will do what they would have done.

Normally the beneficiary designation is revocable. This means that the policyowner retains the right to change the designation.

It is also possible to designate the beneficiary irrevocably, but this arrangement is rarely used. It means that the policyowner cannot change the beneficiary designation without approval of the beneficiary. Nor can the policyowner exercise certain other ownership rights, such as cashing in or borrowing against the policy, without the beneficiary's approval. In effect, then, the policyowner and the irrevocable beneficiary are both part owners of the policy. An irrevocable beneficiary designation may be appropriate in some special situations, such as a divorce, or where a charitable organization is the beneficiary. Under no circumstances, however, should you designate a beneficiary irrevocably without consultation with your attorney.

The disastrous consequences of the improper use of an irrevocable beneficiary designation may be illustrated by the Woodruff case. Mr. and Mrs. Woodruff, owners of a small but successful business, were killed simultaneously in an automobile accident. They were survived by four sons. Jack, the oldest, was 23 when his parents died, and he took over the business. The other three sons were minors. Since the family's financial affairs were in a state of flux following his parents' deaths, Jack bought a substantial straight life policy on his life for the benefit of his three young brothers.

Normally an irrevocable beneficiary designation requires a special written request, but the application in this case had "yes" and "no" boxes following the question about whether the policyowner retains the right to change the beneficiary designation. The agent (who qualified to be Jack's agent because he was Jack's cousin) accidentally checked the "no" box, and Jack signed the application without realizing what he had done. The agent failed to detect the irrevocable designation in the policy and delivered it routinely to Jack.

A few years later, Jack married. By that time, the family's financial affairs had been straightened out, and a trust had been established for the benefit of Jack's brothers. Since there was no further need for the life insurance payable to his brothers, Jack asked the company to designate his new bride as the beneficiary. He was then informed of the irrevocable designation of his brothers. On checking with his attorney, Jack discovered there was no way to effect the change of beneficiary. His brothers, as minors, had no legal capacity to agree to the change, and no judge would stand by and allow minors to have their rights impaired. To add insult to injury, Jack was told that he could neither cash in nor borrow against the policy, since the minors had no legal capacity to agree and no judge would approve such an agreement.

Jack could have continued to pay premiums until his brothers became of age to find out whether they would agree to a beneficiary change. But he decided instead to discontinue premium payments and allow the policy automatically to become extended term insurance (as discussed in Chapter 11). He then had to buy new insurance for the benefit of his bride; fortunately he was insurable and able to do so.

Settlement Options

Settlement options—sometimes called payment options—are the ways in which the beneficiary may receive the funds other than in a single sum. These provisions are complex, and they commonly occupy two full pages in the life insurance contract.

Perhaps the most widely used settlement option is the interest option, sometimes called the deposit option. Here the policy's proceeds are left with the company and interest payments are made to the beneficiary periodically (monthly, quarterly, semiannually, or annually). It is possible to arrange for the beneficiary to have unlimited privileges of withdrawal, or limitations can be imposed. The beneficiary can be given unlimited privileges of changing to another settlement option, or limitations can be imposed.

Another settlement option is the fixed amount option, sometimes called the installment amount option. Here the funds are left with the company and payments of a specified amount, including both principal and interest, are made to the beneficiary periodically until the funds (together with interest) are exhausted. Again, it is usually possible to arrange for the beneficiary to have limited or unlimited privileges of withdrawal and limited or unlimited privileges of changing to another settlement option.

A third settlement option is the fixed period option, sometimes called the installment time option. Here the funds are left with the company and payments including both principal and interest are made to the beneficiary periodically for a specified period of time. Under this option, it may be possible to arrange for the beneficiary to have the privilege of taking all of the remaining funds, but normally the company will not allow the beneficiary to make partial withdrawals.

All three of these options are described as "not involving life contingencies." This expression means that neither the amount of the payments nor the number of payments is contingent upon the survival of the beneficiary. If the first beneficiary dies before receiving all of the funds, the remainder is paid to the next beneficiary in line. With regard to these three options, the important factors are the withdrawal privileges and the interest rates.

Settlement options usually guarantee a minimum interest rate ranging from 2 to 4 percent. Companies then declare additional interest from time to time in accordance with current economic conditions. When a person is considering the use of settlement options, he or she should inquire about interest rates, because these rates vary substantially from company to company and sometimes from one option to another within the same company.

In addition to the options that do not involve life contingencies, most policies provide for at least two or three options involving life contingencies. The latter are the various kinds of life annuities that the beneficiary may receive. One of them, for example, might provide the beneficiary (who we will assume is a woman aged 70) $7.17 per month for life for each $1,000 of proceeds, but in no event for less than ten years. This means that if she dies before receiving 120 monthly payments, the company must continue the payments to the next beneficiary in line until a total of 120 monthly payments have been made. On the other hand, if she lives to receive the 120 monthly payments, the company must continue the payments until she dies.

Two points should be mentioned about life annuities. First, they rarely fit into a financial plan unless the beneficiary is at least 65 or 70 years of age. At younger ages, it is normally preferable to invest the proceeds in high-rated corporate or government bonds, on which the beneficiary would receive the interest while preserving the principal.

Second, the selection of a life annuity option is the same as the purchase of a single-premium life annuity. As such, it is a big purchase that should be made carefully. Suppose, for example, the settlement option rates are more favorable to the beneficiary than current single-premium life annuity rates. Under these circumstances, the settlement option rates should be used.

On the other hand, suppose the settlement option rates are inferior to a company's current single-premium life annuity rates. In this situation, some companies will give the beneficiary the benefit of the better rates, and some of these companies provide a discount from their current rates. But other companies are willing to let the beneficiary suffer the consequences if he or she unknowingly elects a life annuity settlement option when the company's current single-premium life annuity rates would have been more favorable.

Nor is such a questionable practice the only consideration. Some companies are more aggressive and competitive in the single-premium life annuity business than others. It is possible, therefore, that the beneficiary who wants a life annuity would be well advised to take the funds and buy a single-premium life annuity from another company.

One additional point should be mentioned concerning the fixed amount, fixed period, and life annuity options. Each of these involves liquidation of both principal and interest. If the funds arise from the death of the insured, the beneficiary is the insured's spouse, and one of these liquidating options is selected, the beneficiary would be entitled to a $1,000 annual interest exclusion on his or her federal income tax return. In other words, the first $1,000 per year of interest received by the beneficiary under one of these liquidating options would be excluded from the beneficiary's income for federal income tax purposes. This point may be a consideration if the beneficiary has enough income to make the tax benefit attractive.

With the exception of the interest option, which a beneficiary may use temporarily until he or she decides how to manage the funds, settlement options are not widely used. When the amount of life insurance is small from the beneficiary's point of view, he or she may prefer to put the funds into a savings account for simplicity. When the amount of life insurance is large, the beneficiary should be sensitive to interest rates, and should consider a range of investment alternatives, one of which might be a life annuity option.

Even more important, when large amounts are involved, it is often essential to provide for flexibility and discretion. Suppose, for example, you have $100,000 of life insurance payable to your spouse, and you are considering settlement options. If you give your beneficiary the right to withdraw all or most of the funds, he or she might become the victim of bad investments, untrustworthy advisors, or both. On the other hand, if you impose severe restrictions on your beneficiary's right of access to the funds, he or she may have a desperate need for money because of an illness or other emergency. The insurance company cannot exercise discretion in the distribution of funds to your beneficiary; any restrictions imposed through the settlement options are normally unbreakable. Instead of using settlement options, therefore, you may be forced to have the funds payable to a trustee, in whom you can lodge discretion through your will and a trust agreement.

The unbreakable nature of settlement options and the need to review settlement agreements are illustrated by the case of the Johnson family. Mr. Johnson bought a $5,000 policy in 1929, and designated his wife as the beneficiary. In 1941 he executed a settlement agreement providing for his wife to receive the funds under a life annuity settlement option. She was to receive about $30 per month for life (supplemented once each year by some additional interest), but in no event for less than twenty years. Mr. Johnson died in 1977, at which time Mrs. Johnson was aged 91. The 1941 agreement had never been changed. Mrs. Johnson and her family asked the company to pay the proceeds to her in a single lump sum, so that she could have the use of the funds, and to avoid the inconvenience of negotiating a small check each month. However, the company was convinced that it had no choice but to honor the ancient agreement. The company denied the request, and probably would have been upheld if Mrs. Johnson had gone to court.

Ownership Rights and Assignment

Among the ownership rights in a life insurance policy are the right to name and change the beneficiary designation, the right to select and change settlement options, the right to cash in or borrow against the policy, the right to receive any dividends paid by the company, and the right to dispose of some or all of the policy ownership rights. When a person possesses all the ownership rights in a policy, that person is the sole owner. (If a person possesses some of the rights, that person is a part owner.) In most instances, the insured and the owner are the same person. In some policies, however, someone other than the insured is the owner. A typical policy contains several clauses dealing with ownership rights.

If the owner of a policy gives or sells all the ownership rights to someone else, the transaction is known as a transfer of ownership or an absolute assignment. It is also possible for the owner to dispose of some but not all of the ownership rights. Commonly this occurs when the owner wants to pledge the policy to a financial institution as collateral for a loan, in which case the transaction is known as a collateral assignment.

The assignment clause is important because it gives the life insurance contract flexibility that it would not otherwise have. Perhaps the classic example of widely used financial instruments that lack assignability are United States savings bonds, which are identified on their face as nontransferable.

Should you ever have occasion to assign a life insurance policy as collateral for a bank loan, be sure that the assignment form you execute is the ABA assignment form. This is a document worked out by the American Bankers Association in consultation with representatives of the life insurance industry. Under the ABA form, you give the bank just enough of the ownership rights to protect its interests. Before the ABA form was developed, banks prepared their own assignment forms, under which they sometimes received more ownership rights than necessary to protect their interests. In some instances, they received all the ownership rights. The reason for this warning is that some financial institutions still use their own assignment forms, the terms of which may be less favorable to the borrower than those of the ABA form.

Grace Period

Life insurance contracts provide a grace period—usually thirty-one days—beyond the premium due dates. The policy continues in force during the grace period. If the insured dies during the grace period without having paid the premium, the unpaid premium would be deducted from the death benefit otherwise payable under the policy. If the company follows the practice of refunding at death the unearned portion of the premium (as discussed earlier), only one month's premium would be deducted from the death benefit otherwise payable under the policy.

Grace period clauses generally are silent on the question of interest from the premium due date, but companies usually forget about the interest when the premium is paid during the grace period. It is difficult administratively for the company to collect such interest, because the amount of interest due cannot be determined until the exact date of payment is known. On the other hand, some companies charge interest for the grace period when the premium is paid in part or in full by the use of the automatic premium loan provision, discussed in Chapter 11.

Incontestability

Under the incontestability clause the company cannot "contest" the policy after it has been in force for two years. (In a few companies the period is one year.) The clause may be worded as follows:

> We must bring any legal action to contest the validity of this policy within two years from its issue date. After that we cannot contest its validity, except for failure to pay premiums.

This policy provision is crucial. In the absence of such a clause, the company could deny a death claim, many years after the policy was issued, on the grounds that the insured made a misstatement in the original application. For example, the insured may have made a misstatement about his or her medical history. The company could deny the claim even though the misstatement may have been inadvertent or not significant. Such a denial might create difficulties for the beneficiary, not only because the insured is not alive to argue the case, but also because the beneficiary might be in need of funds and thus at a disadvantage in a protracted legal dispute.

Over the years, the courts have broadened the effect of the clause to protect a beneficiary even when the insured apparently made fraudulent statements to obtain the insurance. About the only circumstances in which insurance companies have been able to get around the clause are those where the fraud is outrageous, as when a policy is taken out with the intent to murder the insured. In other words, the incontestability clause is a powerful form of protection for the beneficiary.

It is important, however, to distinguish between a contest and a denial of a claim under a policy provision. Suppose, for example, a policy is issued with an aviation restriction, under which the company does not have to pay the death benefit if the insured dies in the crash of a private plane he or she was piloting. When the company denies the payment of this type of claim, it is merely following a policy provision—the aviation restriction. Such a denial is not a "contest" and is not affected by the incontestability clause.

Suicide

The insuring agreement states that the company will pay the death benefit upon receipt of due proof of the insured's death. In the absence of a clause to the contrary, the company would have to pay even if death resulted from suicide. To relieve the companies from paying death claims on behalf of insureds who buy life insurance with the intent to commit suicide, the contracts contain a suicide clause. That clause reduces the liability of the companies to a return of the premiums if suicide occurs within two years (or, in a few policies, one year) of the issue date of the policy. The wording of the suicide clause may be as follows:

> If the insured commits suicide, while sane or insane, within two years from the issue date, and while this policy is in force, we will pay a limited death benefit in one sum to the beneficiary. The limited death benefit will be the amount of premiums paid for this policy, less any policy debt.

The suicide clause also makes sense from the standpoint of public policy. In the absence of the restriction, the availability of the life insurance contract could be an inducement to suicide. For example, if a man were seriously depressed, the financial plight of his family in the event of his death might be the one thing that would prevent him from committing suicide. If he could buy life insurance without a suicide restriction, he might do so and then promptly commit suicide.

Reinstatement

When a premium is not paid by the end of the grace period, and when the automatic premium loan provision (discussed in Chapter 11) is not operative, the policy lapses. The reinstatement clause spells out the requirements that have to be met for the policy to be reinstated. Here is how the reinstatement clause might be worded:

> The policy lapses at the end of the grace period. It may be reinstated during the lifetime of the insured and within five years after the due date of the unpaid premium. Within fifteen days after the end of the grace period and during the lifetime of the insured, the policy may be reinstated by payment of the overdue premium. After fifteen days after the end of the grace period, reinstatement is subject to (a) evidence of insurability satisfactory to us, and (b) payment of all overdue premiums with interest from the due date of each premium. The interest rate is 6 percent per

annum, compounded annually. Any policy indebtedness existing on the due date of the unpaid premium, with interest from that date, must be repaid or reinstated.

Misstatement of Age

When the insured dies, a discrepancy is sometimes found between the age of the insured at death and the age given in the application for insurance. In this situation, the misstatement-of-age clause provides that the death benefit be adjusted to what the premium would have bought at the correct age. Here is how the misstatement-of-age clause might be worded:

> One of the questions in the application concerns the insured's date of birth. If the date of birth given is not correct, all benefits and amounts payable under this policy will be what the premiums paid would have bought if the correct date of birth had been given.

For example, suppose Steve bought a $100,000 straight life policy at the stated age of 35. The annual premium was $1,600. He died exactly ten years later, at which time he was found to be 46. If the premium paid would have bought a $95,000 policy at age 36, the latter would be the death benefit paid by the insurance company.

The clause also operates in the opposite direction. For example, if Steve was found to be 44 at death, the death benefit paid by the company might be $105,000.

The misstatement-of-age clause seems eminently fair, but it has been subjected to criticism. It has been argued that some companies use the clause only when it operates in their favor. Further, it has been argued that it is unfair for three reasons to base a settlement on the age given in a death certificate. First, such a certificate comes into existence at a time when the insured can no longer challenge it. Second, the age on a death certificate may be an estimate given to a funeral director by a member of the insured's family. Third, the effect of the practice is to place upon the beneficiary the burden of disproving the age on the death certificate. The beneficiary may need the funds quickly, may not be able to secure proof of the insured's age readily, and may be unable to afford the legal expense of fighting a relatively small reduction in the death benefit. Thus, it is argued that some companies use the misstatement-of-age clause to engage in a form of "clipping."*

You can protect your beneficiary against such clipping by filing proof of age with the insurance company during your lifetime. Get the company to acknowledge that such proof is satisfactory, and file the acknowledgment with the policy. Some companies' policies specifically refer to their willingness to receive and acknowledge a proof of age, and other companies probably would do so. Another safeguard is to have a birth certificate or other proof of age safely filed with your valuable papers and to inform your beneficiary where to find these papers.

You should take steps to protect your beneficiary, because a misstatement of age can lead to a substantial reduction in the death benefit. The discrepancy illustrated above was for one year in age. If the discrepancy were five or ten years, the reduction would be a substantial proportion of the death benefit.

Some companies in recent years have expanded the misstatement-of-age clause to include misstatement of sex. The expanded clause provides that, in the event of a misstatement of sex, the death benefit will be adjusted to what the premium would have bought at the correct sex. The clause is relevant because women experience lower death rates than men. Therefore, a woman generally pays a smaller premium than a man who buys the same insurance at the same age.

Alteration of Policy

The alteration clause states that no modification of the policy is valid unless it is accomplished in writing over the signature of a company officer. Here is how the clause might read:

> No agent or other person except our president, a vice-president, or our secretary or assistant secretary has authority to bind us, to extend the time in which you can pay your premiums, or to agree to change this policy. Any such change must be in writing.

---

*See Oscar R. Goodman, "Public Policy and the Age and Incontestable Clauses in Life Insurance Contracts," *Journal of Risk and Insurance*, Vol. XXXV, No. 4 (December, 1968), pp. 515–535; Oscar R. Goodman, "A Statement before the NAIC on Protection of the Public Interest and the Misstatement of Age Clause in Life Insurance Contracts," *Journal of Risk and Insurance*, Vol. XXXVIII, No. 1 (March, 1971), pp. 147–152; and "MONY and the Misstatement-of-Age Clause," *The Insurance Forum*, Vol. 3, No. 9 (September, 1976), pp. 1–2.

The moral is that you should not accept the verbal (or written, for that matter) assurances of an agent. To illustrate, suppose the contract is silent on the question of interest between the date of death and the date of the settlement check. You ask the agent about it, and he or she assures you that the company pays such interest. Do not take the agent's word for it. Insist that the agent obtain for you a letter to that effect over the signature of a company officer, and file the letter with the policy.

Dividend Options

When a policy is participating, the company contemplates the payment of periodic (usually annual) amounts called "dividends." The terminology is unfortunate because the word "dividend" implies the policyowner is receiving something resembling the dividend paid to a corporate shareholder. The terminology developed in the nineteenth century at least in part as a marketing strategy; that is, it made possible a more attractive or "romantic" sales presentation.

One widely held view is that a life insurance policy dividend is a refund of an overcharge built into the policy's premiums. This view is the one that has been adopted in the Internal Revenue Code and is the reason why a life insurance policy dividend is not taxable income to the policyowner. As discussed in Chapter 3, life insurance policy dividends may be viewed in other ways as well.

Regardless of how they are viewed, dividends are simply periodic payments to policyowners, and companies usually offer their policyowners a variety of ways in which to use the dividends. In some sales interviews, the discussion of dividend options consumes a disproportionate amount of time, perhaps because it is pleasant to talk about dividends and unpleasant to talk about death.

One dividend option is payment in cash. The policyowner receives a check each year for the amount of the dividend.

Another option is to use the dividend to reduce the premium. The dividend is applied against the premium due, and the premium notice bills the policyowner for the difference between the premium and the dividend.

Both these options result in the policyowner's immediate receipt of the dividend. The other options require the policyowner to leave the dividends with the company.

A third option is to leave the dividends with the company to accumulate at interest. The result is the establishment of a savings account. The contract usually guarantees a minimum interest rate ranging from 2 to 4 percent. Companies then declare additional interest from time to time in accordance with their current earnings. In the event of the insured's death, dividend accumulations are paid to the beneficiary in addition to the policy's basic death benefit; in the event that the policyowner cashes in the policy, the dividend accumulations are paid to the policyowner in addition to the cash value. The accumulation may be withdrawn in whole or in part by the policyowner at any time, but normally cannot be redeposited. The interest on the dividend accumulation is taxable in the year earned just as is interest on a savings account.

A fourth option is to use dividends to buy "paid-up additions" to the basic policy. This means that each dividend is used to buy a small single-premium life insurance addition to the basic policy. The amount of the paid-up addition is determined by the amount of the dividend, the age of the insured at the time the dividend is payable, and the company's premium rates for paid-up additions.

One advantage of paid-up additions relative to dividend accumulations relates to income taxation. As indicated earlier, the interest on dividend accumulations is taxable to the policyowner in the year earned. In paid-up additions, however, the income tax treatment of the inside interest is the same as for any other cash-value life insurance. (That treatment was discussed in Chapter 5.)

Another advantage of paid-up additions is that they are available without evidence of insurability. Therefore, they are advantageous to an individual who is no longer insurable, or who can qualify for life insurance only at a high rate.

It is sometimes said that another advantage of paid-up additions is that they are a low-priced form of insurance. This statement may or may not be true. The only way to find out is from a price analysis of paid-up additions. In one such study several years ago, it was found that the paid-up additions offered by some companies were indeed low-priced, while the paid-up additions offered by other companies were high-priced.*

---

*Joseph M. Belth, *The Retail Price Structure in American Life Insurance* (Bloomington, IN: Indiana University School of Business, 1966), pp. 124–127.

Aside from the possibility that the paid-up additions offered by a given company may be high-priced, another disadvantage of this option is that single-premium life insurance is rarely appropriate. If you want $100,000 of life insurance, would you pay a single premium of $40,000 to get it? If not, why would you use a $40 dividend to buy a $100 paid-up addition? As stated earlier, the life insurance needs of most individuals can be met satisfactorily with one-year renewable term, straight life, or some combination of the two. Both of these are annual-premium rather than single-premium forms of life insurance.

A few companies offer a "full term addition" option. Here the dividend is used to buy one-year term insurance. The death benefit of the term addition is determined by the amount of the dividend, the age of the insured at the time the dividend is payable, and the company's premium rates on term additions. If you consider selecting this option, you should check on the price of the additions, using the procedure described in Chapter 8. Unlike paid-up additions, the one-year term form of insurance often is appropriate. It is not uncommon for a $40 dividend to buy $20,000 or more of one-year term protection for young insureds. It is unfortunate that the option is not offered by more companies.

Many companies offer one or more "split term addition" options that are some combination of the full term addition option and another option. For example, many companies offer an option under which part of the dividend is used to buy one-year term insurance equal to the basic policy's cash value. The remainder of the dividend is left with the company to accumulate at interest or is applied under another option.

The simplest decision is to take each dividend as it arises, either in cash or by applying it to the premium then payable. This approach is satisfactory if you have purchased the amount of life insurance you need and if you plan to review your needs frequently.

On the other hand, you may prefer to leave your dividends with the company. For example, you may want to use additions to increase your life insurance automatically. The material in this section will help you understand the options available to you.

Chapter 10

Contract Provisions in One-Year Renewable Term Policies

It is sometimes said that one-year renewable term policies are simple in comparison with straight life policies, but there are some significant complexities in term policies. This chapter contains discussions of several contract provisions found in one-year renewable term policies.

Renewability

The duration of a one-year renewable term policy is one year, at the end of which the policy expires. The renewal provision describes the way in which you may continue the policy for additional one-year terms without having to requalify. This provision is important and should be examined in any policy you are considering. You should purchase a one-year renewable term policy only if it is renewable at least to the age of 65.

Some term policies are not renewable. This means that the coverage expires at the end of the term, and the only way you can continue the coverage is to purchase new insurance. You then have to go through the regular qualification process. The renewability feature has substantial value, and costs money. Therefore, you should expect to pay a higher price for a renewable term policy than for an otherwise comparable nonrenewable term policy. Do not let someone talk you into buying nonrenewable term to save a few dollars. Since it is impossible for you to forecast the future as far as your life insurance needs and your state of health are concerned, spend the extra money for the renewability feature.

Premiums

Under one-year renewable term policies, the premium increases each year the policy is renewed for an additional one-year term. In most policies, the future premiums that will be charged are shown in the contract. In some policies, however, future premiums are not shown. Avoid buying a one-year renewable term policy in which the future premiums are not shown.

Some policies—often called "indeterminate premium" policies—show maximum premiums and provide that the premiums charged may be less than the maximum premiums shown. From the buyer's point of view, such policies are essentially the same as participating policies in which the dividends—which are not guaranteed—are used to reduce the premiums. If you consider buying such a policy, therefore, treat it as you would a participating policy. (See Chapter 3.)

Reentry

Some one-year renewable term policies contain a reentry provision, under which there are two possible premium levels in the future. One level of rates applies if you qualify in the future by providing the company with satisfactory evidence of insurability. A higher level of rates applies if you fail to requalify in the future.

The concept of reeentry sounds good—if you stay in good shape, the insurance company will reward you with lower premiums in the future. Someone who tries to sell you on the concept is likely to place considerable emphasis on the lower premium level.

The concept is open to question. First, it is often not clear what you will have to do to meet the requirements for the favorable future rates. Second, the concept means that if you develop some kind of health difficulty in the future, your problems will be compounded by the obligation to pay higher premiums to keep the policy in force. If you consider a policy with a reentry provision, evaluate the price of the policy on the assumption that you will fail to qualify for the lower premium level in the future.

Grace Period

The grace period was discussed in Chapter 9. A special problem may exist in one-year renewable term policies, because technically the coverage expires at the end of each year. The question, then, is whether the coverage continues in effect for thirty-one days following the expiration date if the premium for the subsequent year is not paid on time.

Most one-year renewable term policies specify in the contract that the coverage remains in force during the thirty-one days following expiration of the term period. In other words, a grace period for the subsequent premium is allowed in such policies just as it is in continuous policies such as straight life.

Some policies, however, are not clear on this point. Be sure to check. The problem may not affect you if you follow the practice of paying premiums on or before their due dates. But if you follow the practice of using all or part of the grace period, it is possible that a one-year term policy will not cover you during the period of up to thirty-one days following the expiration of each one-year term. If you die during this period, it can be disastrous for your beneficiary.

The significance of a technical point such as this one is illustrated by an incident that occurred during the preparation of the first edition of this book. A survey of policy provisions showed that the policies of several companies did not make this particular point clear. In response to a letter of inquiry, an official of one company stated—in writing—that the coverage was not in effect during the thirty-one days following the expiration of the term coverage. After the book was published, another official of the same company stated—in writing—that the individual who had written earlier had made a mistake, and that the coverage was indeed in effect during the thirty-one days after expiration of the term coverage. The question is whether a similar mistake could be made in the claims process.

It is sometimes difficult to determine when you are getting incorrect information. Therefore, do not hesitate to challenge an adverse decision by the company when you have reason to doubt its correctness. The procedure for filing a complaint with your state insurance department is described in Chapter 15.

Convertibility

The conversion clause describes how you may exchange your one-year renewable term policy for some other type of policy without evidence of insurability. Virtually all one-year renewable term policies contain conversion clauses, but you must examine the clause to determine for how many years the policy is convertible. You should consider purchasing a one-year renewable term policy only if it is convertible at least to the age of 60.

You can convert in one of two ways. One is called an "attained age conversion." The new policy is written as of the time of conversion. The premium for the new policy is based on your age at the time of conversion, and the policy form is of the type written by the company at that time. This form of conversion is the most common and is provided for in all convertible term policies.

The other is called an "original age conversion." Here the new policy is written as of the issue date of the term policy. The premium is based on your age when you bought the term policy. To obtain the lower premium rate, however, a financial adjustment is necessary at the time of conversion. For example, you may have to pay the company a sum equal to the differences in premiums since the issue date of the term policy, together with 5 or 6 percent interest compounded annually on these differences. Some term policies do not offer this type of conversion, and those that do usually limit the period (sometimes to five years) within which such a conversion may be made. In any case, the size of the financial adjustment represents a major barrier to an original age conversion. Thus, few policyowners use this form of conversion.

After you purchase a one-year renewable term policy, you may be urged to convert the policy into straight life or some other type of policy that builds cash values. Unfortunately, some of the tactics used by companies and agents in an effort to convince policyowners to exercise the conversion privilege are deceptive. Do not convert your policy without an analysis of the price and suitability of the policy you would acquire. To make these determinations, you should follow the procedures described in this book.

Incontestability and Suicide

The incontestability and suicide clauses were discussed in Chapter 9. The process of converting a one-year renewable term policy, how-ever, creates some additional considerations regarding these clauses.

To illustrate, consider a hypothetical case. Tom buys a one-year renewable term policy on July 1, 1985. He converts to straight life at his attained age exactly three years later—on July 1, 1988. Then, on February 1, 1989, Tom dies. The questions are these: Is the policy contestable? And is the suicide restriction in effect? The answer to both questions would have been no if Tom had chosen to continue the term policy rather than converting it, because the two-year period of contestability and the two-year suicide exclusion would have expired. But Tom did convert, and he paid the increased premium for the straight life policy on July 1, 1988.

The question about incontestability is academic. When Tom con-verted, no evidence of insurability was required; therefore, with no questions having been asked and no answers having been given, no basis for a contest exists.

The question about suicide, however, is far from academic. If Tom's death were the result of suicide, and if the suicide period of the new policy were measured from the date of conversion, the com-pany's liability would be limited to a return of the premiums paid on the new policy. On the other hand, if the suicide period were meas-ured from the issue date of the original term policy, the company's liability would be the full death benefit of the policy.

Some term policies provide specifically for the incontestability and suicide clauses of a new policy to be endorsed so that the periods run from the issue date of the original term policy. But some term policies are silent on this point. In the survey referred to earlier, some com-pany officials said their companies follow the practice of endorsing the new policy so that the contestability and suicide periods run from the issue date of the original term policy. Further, some company officials said the companies would be hard pressed—legally, morally, and on the basis of common sense—to invoke the suicide exclusion in this situation. Such comments are encouraging, but they would be of little consolation to Tom's beneficiaries if he converted the term policy, if the company failed to endorse the new policy, if Tom then committed suicide, and if the company's liability was limited to a return of the premiums paid on the new policy.

One company official—indicating his company followed the practice of endorsing the new policy—suggested the point should be irrelevant for a policyowner acting in good faith. He even implied his company would be wary about issuing a term policy in the first place to a person who would inquire about this point. The attitude of this official is appalling. His company was issuing a policy with an important point left hanging, and he said an applicant who asks for clarification would be viewed with suspicion and perhaps denied coverage for having the temerity to inquire.

Check this point if you buy a one-year renewable term policy. If the company you are considering does not provide in its term policy that it will endorse a new policy, and if it follows the practice of endorsing the new policy upon conversion, it should be willing to guarantee by letter that it will endorse the new policy. On the other hand, if the company does not provide in its term policy that it will endorse a new policy, and if it does not follow the practice of endorsing the new policy upon conversion, you are then forewarned about the possibility of a new suicide exclusion period under the new policy.

The preceding discussion refers to the distinction between a policy provision and company practice. The company is obligated to do what a policy provision says will be done. However, as a general rule the company is not obligated to continue a company practice. For that reason, be wary when important aspects of the coverage are dealt with as a matter of practice rather than through policy provisions.

Waiver of Premium

The waiver-of-premium clause, under which premiums are waived in the event of the total and permanent disability of the insured, was discussed in Chapter 3. When the clause is attached to a one-year renewable term policy, companies follow various practices concerning the inclusion of the clause in a new policy obtained through conversion of the term policy.

Suppose Bill buys a one-year renewable term policy with a waiver-of-premium clause, converts the term policy a few years later to straight life at his attained age, is not disabled at the time of conversion, and desires to include the waiver-of-premium clause in the new policy. Some companies will not allow inclusion of the waiver-of-premium clause in the new policy unless the insured provides evidence of insurability. Some companies allow inclusion of the clause without evidence of insurability, but provide that the clause is operative only with respect to disabilities that are not the result of an injury sustained or disease contracted before the date of conversion. Some companies allow inclusion of the clause without evidence of insurability only if conversion is made before age 55, thus effectively shortening the period of conversion if Bill wants to have the clause included in the new policy without evidence of insurability. And some companies allow inclusion of the clause without evidence of insurability, without a preexisting conditions clause, and without an additional age restriction. The practice of the last group of companies is the most desirable for the consumer. Examine this point in any one-year renewable term policy you are considering.

Now suppose Bill buys a one-year renewable term policy with a waiver-of-premium clause, becomes totally and permanently disabled a few years later, and wants to convert to straight life at his attained age. Will he be able to obtain the waiver-of-premium clause in the straight life policy without evidence of insurability?

Some companies provide that the waiver-of-premium clause may be included in the straight life policy only if conversion is postponed until some specified age. The specified age usually is 55 or older. In these companies, if Bill wants to convert immediately after becoming disabled or at some other point before the specified minimum age, the waiver-of-premium clause is not included in the new straight life policy. This provision discourages conversion by disabled individuals, because premiums are waived if the policy is continued as term insurance but are not waived if the policy is converted to straight life.

Some companies, however, allow Bill to convert at any time within the conversion period and include the waiver-of-premium clause in the new straight life policy without evidence of insurability. This approach is more desirable for the consumer. Conversion by disabled individuals is encouraged, because the higher premiums for the straight life policy are waived and the cash values accumulate for the benefit of the policyowner.

Summary

Some of the points in this chapter appear complex. At the same time, they can be important, and the buyer of a one-year renewable term policy should be aware of them. By way of summary, the following is a list of questions that should be answered before you buy a one-year renewable term policy:

- To what age may coverage be continued without evidence of insurability?
- Is the premium rate for each year specified in the contract?
- If the insured dies within thirty-one days after the expiration of a one-year term, and if the premium for at least part of the next one-year term has not been paid, will the insurance protection still be in effect?
- To what age can the policy be converted to straight life at attained age without evidence of insurability?
- Does the one-year renewable term contract guarantee that, if the insured converts to straight life at attained age, the incontestability and suicide clauses in the straight life policy will be modified to provide that the periods run from the issue date of the term policy?
- If the insured is not disabled at the time of conversion, and if the insured converts to straight life at attained age, will the waiver-of-premium clause be included in the straight life policy without evidence of insurability?
- If the insured is disabled at the time of conversion, and if the insured converts to straight life at attained age, will the waiver-of-premium clause be included in the straight life policy without evidence of insurability?

Chapter 11

Contract Provisions in Cash-Value Policies

Some of the provisions found in cash-value policies were discussed in Chapter 9 because those provisions are found in life insurance policies generally. This chapter contains discussions of several contract provisions that are peculiar to cash-value policies.

The Loan Clause

Cash-value life insurance policies invariably contain a clause allowing the policyowner to borrow against the policy. It was mentioned in Chapter 5 that the loan clause makes the savings component of a cash-value policy a liquid asset for the policyowner. It is important for the policyowner to understand how the clause operates.

The maximum amount that can be borrowed is approximately the cash value of the policy at the time of the loan minus interest for the remainder of the current policy year. To illustrate, consider the hypothetical $100,000 straight life policy for which raw data are shown in Table 3 on page 27. Suppose the policy loan interest rate (to be discussed later) is 8 percent, the annual premium for the fifth year has been paid, and the policyowner wants to know the maximum loan available in the middle of the fifth year.

At the end of the fifth year, the cash value is $5,000. The maximum loan available is $5,000 minus interest for the remainder of the fifth year. To calculate the figure, you must first determine what portion of the policy loan interest rate applies to the remainder of the current year. In this illustration, because you are in the middle of the year, exactly half of the policy loan interest rate, or 4 percent, applies to the remainder of the year. Next, divide the $5,000 by $(1 + i)$ where i is the portion of the policy loan interest rate, expressed as a decimal, that applies to the remainder of the year. In this case, the $5,000 is divided by 1.04, and the maximum loan available is $4,808.

The loan clause provides that, with the exception of loans used to pay premiums on the company's policies, the company may postpone making a loan for up to six months. This provision is similar to the delay clause found in savings accounts. Both were instituted as a result of the traumatic bank runs of the Great Depression. The delay clause is rarely used by life insurance companies; the potentially disastrous public relations effect of invoking it is likely to deter companies from using it except under the most extreme circumstances.*

In the event that the insured dies with a loan outstanding against the policy, the amount of the loan, together with any unpaid interest,

---

*For a discussion of the delay clause and a situation in which it was invoked, see "The Delay Clause Rears Its Ugly Head," *The Insurance Forum*, Vol. 4, No. 3 (March, 1977), pp. 1–2.

is deducted from the death benefit payable to the beneficiary. Similarly, in the event that a loan is outstanding at the time the policyowner cashes in the policy, the amount of the loan, together with any unpaid interest, is deducted from the cash value payable to the policyowner. With these exceptions, there is no requirement for repayment of the loan. The policyowner can pay off the loan in full whenever he or she wants, partial payments can be made at any time (usually a minimum limit is imposed, such as $10), or the policyowner can make no payments.

This lack of a payment requirement has been described accurately both as an advantage and as a disadvantage of policy loans. On the one hand, it is good to be free from pressure to pay. On the other hand, the absence of pressure makes payment less likely and consequently may disrupt the systematic savings feature of cash-value life insurance.

Until recent years, life insurance policies usually specified a fixed policy loan interest rate—most commonly either 5 or 6 percent. When market interest rates were low, the fixed policy loan interest rate worked satisfactorily. During the 1970s and the early 1980s, however, when market interest rates rose rapidly, the life insurance companies were confronted with serious problems. Many policyowners borrowed large sums of money at 5 or 6 percent from the companies and invested them at the higher market interest rates. This practice deprived the insurance companies of a large portion of the funds they expected to have available for investment at high market interest rates. Instead they were forced to make loans to their policyowners at below-market interest rates.

This problem was not a minor one. For some life insurance companies—including some of the giants—the policy loan demand was so great that their usual strongly positive cash flow was converted into a strongly negative cash flow. To deal with the problem, these companies had to either liquidate some of their assets (mainly bonds, whose market value was depressed because of high market interest rates) or borrow from banks at high market interest rates. Such companies also had to curtail drastically their commitments to make long-term investments. In the spring of 1980, market interest rates rose so sharply and to such high levels that some life insurance companies faced a full-scale financial crisis.

The crisis subsided as market interest rates declined. The companies, fearful of possible future market interest rate instability, have taken steps to reduce their exposure. They have lobbied for changes in state insurance laws to allow the use of variable policy loan interest rates in newly issued policies. Nearly all states now allow such provisions, and many new policies now issued include variable loan interest rates. In most cases, the clause provides that the company may change the policy loan interest rate from time to time in accordance with an index of market interest rates.

Some policies issued currently still carry fixed policy loan interest rates of 6 or 8 percent, and some policies provide for variable policy loan interest rates with a maximum rate, such as 8 percent. Some of the companies that issue such policies, however, provide that the dividends on their policies will be determined in part by policy loan activity. In other words, if market interest rates are higher than the policy loan interest rate, and if you borrow against your policy, the dividend on your policy will be smaller than it would have been had you not borrowed against your policy. If the company you are considering follows this practice, you should obtain two dividend illustrations—one based on the assumption that you do not borrow against the policy, and another based on the assumption that you borrow heavily against the policy.

These company actions on newly issued policies, however, do not solve their problems of large loan values in existing policies with fixed policy loan interest rates. For existing policies, some companies have approached their policyowners with various offers in an effort to amend their policies. If you are approached to amend an existing policy, study the details of the offer before you agree to accept it.

Another issue is how the loan interest rate is expressed. The loan clause in some policies states that interest will be at the rate of, say, 6 percent, and uses such language as "will be due and payable at the end of each policy year," or "will be due and payable annually, not in advance." In such policies, if $100 is borrowed at the beginning of the year and repaid at the end of the year, $6 interest is also payable at the end of the year. Since the policyowner has the use of $100 for a year and pays $6 interest at the end of the year, the effective annual policy loan interest rate is 6 percent ($6 divided by $100).

Some policies, however, state that interest will be at the rate of 6 percent "payable in advance." Let's again assume that $100 is borrowed at the beginning of the year and repaid at the end of the year. In this case, however, the company takes the $6 interest at the beginning of the year, and the policyowner receives $94. At the end of the year, the policyowner pays $100. Thus, the policyowner in effect pays $6 at the end of the year for the use of $94 for the year, and the effective annual policy loan interest rate is about 6.4 percent ($6 divided by $94).

If the life insurance companies are ever required to comply with the federal truth-in-lending legislation enacted in 1969, they will have to disclose the effective annual interest rate on policy loans. Meanwhile, the wording of the loan clause must be examined to ascertain the effective annual policy loan interest rate.

Automatic Premium Loans

Most cash-value policies now include an automatic premium loan (APL) clause. The clause is operative only if it has been elected by the policyowner. The election may be made when the policy is applied for, or at some later date. When operative, the clause commits the company to make a policy loan automatically for the purpose of paying a premium that is not paid by the end of the grace period, provided the policy contains a loan value sufficient to handle the premium then due. No charge is levied by the company for the clause itself.

The APL clause can be both valuable and convenient, but it also can be troublesome. It can be valuable because the policy is automatically kept in force even though a premium may have been left unpaid inadvertently by the policyowner. In the absence of APL, the policy would lapse and would require reinstatement to be back in full force.

It can be convenient because the policyowner may not have the funds readily available to pay a premium, and the APL clause means that he or she will not have to go through the mechanics of obtaining a regular policy loan. Similarly, the policyowner may have readily available only enough to pay part of the premium, in which case he or she can send in that portion and indicate on the premium notice that the balance is to be handled through the APL clause.

The clause can be troublesome, however, because a policyowner may come to rely too heavily upon it. The policyowner may develop the habit of allowing premiums to be paid by APL, and this may tend to destroy the long-term systematic savings feature of cash-value life insurance.

Despite this troublesome aspect, usually it is desirable to elect the APL clause. You should familiarize yourself with it, however. Some companies allow only one or two consecutive premiums to be handled by APL, while others allow an unlimited number of premiums to be handled by APL.

When a premium is paid by APL, the result is essentially the same as though the policyowner had borrowed under the loan clause and used the funds to pay the premium. The only exception to this generalization is that some companies charge interest on automatic premium loans beginning on the premium due date, although other companies charge interest beginning at the end of the grace period. When interest is measured from the premium due date, the effect is to charge interest during the grace period, a charge which otherwise would not be made. This may be a minor point; for example, one month's interest on an annual premium of $1,200 paid by APL, with a policy loan interest rate of 8 percent, is only about $8. It illustrates, however, how money is sometimes extracted from policyowners in ways that are nearly invisible.

Nonforfeiture Options

An understanding of nonforfeiture options requires some explanation. The explanation, in turn, involves a discussion of some life insurance fundamentals.

Death rates (or mortality rates) are the raw materials from which life insurance is fashioned. A mortality table is a device used by life insurance companies in many of their calculations and is developed by observing death rates among a large number of people at various ages.

For example, suppose a mortality table shows a death rate of .00118 among men aged 35. This means that out of 100,000 men aged 35 the expectation is that 118 will die within one year. Now suppose an insurance company wants to sell a $1,000 one-year term life insurance policy to each of the 100,000 men aged 35. Because 118 of the men are expected to die within one year, and because the insurance company will have to pay $1,000 to the beneficiary of each of the deceased men, the insurance company expects to pay out a total of $118,000. Disregarding the timing of deaths and the timing of the insurance company's receipts during the year, it would be necessary for each of the 100,000 men to pay $1.18 to cover the expected mortality costs of the $1,000 one-year term policy.

Death rates, and therefore the mortality costs of life insurance, increase rapidly with age. For example, Table 10 shows some of the death rates in a recent mortality table based on the combined experience of a group of large life insurance companies. While it would take only $1.18 per $1,000 to cover the expected mortality costs for men at age 35, it would take $3.19 at age 45, $8.28 at age 55, $21.52 at age 65, and so on. Because the insurance company must add enough to the premiums to take care of its expenses and make a profit, it would be necessary for each man to pay more than these amounts.

Table 10
Death Rates at Various Ages

Age	Death Rate	
	Males	Females
25	.00108	.00053
35	.00118	.00082
45	.00319	.00237
55	.00828	.00526
65	.02152	.01145
75	.05635	.03199
85	.13533	.10110

Source: From the 1980 Commissioners Standard Ordinary basic mortality table as published by the Society of Actuaries.

Now suppose a person buys a one-year renewable term life insurance policy. The premiums for this policy increase as the insured ages, in a manner similar to the increase in mortality rates.

These increasing premiums may be disconcerting to the policyowner, and they also present a difficult problem for the insurance company. The problem stems from an increasingly strong tendency for healthy persons to discontinue their insurance as the premium becomes higher and higher and for unhealthy individuals to continue their coverage. The result is a tendency for the remaining group to "deteriorate." This phenomenon is referred to in life insurance as "adverse selection" because it leads to a higher level of death payments, relative to premium payments, than would be the case in the absence of adverse selection.

To overcome adverse selection, at least to some extent, and to keep premiums down in the later years, insurance companies devised an arrangement under which premiums remain unchanged as the insured grows older. This level-premium arrangement requires higher premiums in the early policy years than would be paid under one-year renewable term, to make up for lower premiums in the later policy years. For example, excluding interest, the level annual premium for each $1,000 of straight life issued to 35-year-old men would be $24.29. This figure is based upon the mortality table from which excerpts are shown in Table 10, and would cover just the expected mortality costs of the policy.

Because the life insurance policy usually is a long-term financial instrument, the interest factor plays a crucial and powerful role. Consider the foregoing level premium of $24.29, which is calculated without the interest factor. When 6 percent interest is used in the calculations, the level annual premium drops to $7.83. Again, this covers just the expected mortality costs, and would have to be increased to permit the insurance company to cover its expenses and profit.

The insurance company's promises under a life insurance policy are conditioned upon the payment of premiums, but policyowners are not required to pay premiums. They are free to discontinue premium payments at any time, and many do. Under a one-year renewable term policy, with its increasing premiums, the policyowner who discontinues premium payments receives no cash value. The policyowner has paid for and received protection, just as in the case of a homeowner's insurance policy or an automobile insurance policy.

Under a level-premium life insurance policy, however, the policyowner pays more in the early policy years than he or she would pay under one-year renewable term. When the policyowner discontinues premium payments under a level-premium policy, it is reasonable that he or she should receive a cash-value payment from the insurance company and that the amount of the payment should represent roughly the amount of the overpayment (including interest). The word "roughly" is used here because it is necessary to adjust the cash value, particularly in the early policy years, to compensate for the expenses incurred by the company in issuing the policy.

In the early days of life insurance in the United States, companies often paid nothing when a policyowner discontinued a level-premium policy. Critics of this practice argued that the policyowner was forced by the company to "forfeit" the overpayments that had been made relative to what would have been paid if the policyowner had bought one-year renewable term. The laws introduced to require cash values for terminating policyowners were thus called "nonforfeiture laws." Similarly, the various ways in which terminating policyowners could obtain their cash values were called "nonforfeiture options" or "nonforfeiture values."

The typical straight life policy has three nonforfeiture options. One, the cash value, is the single sum that the policyowner may receive when he or she terminates the policy. The cash values available at various points in the life of the policy are shown in a table of nonforfeiture values included in the policy.

Another nonforfeiture option is paid-up insurance. Here the policyowner uses the cash value as a single premium to buy a paid-up life insurance policy. The death benefit of the paid-up policy usually is far below the death benefit of the original straight life policy and is determined by the amount of the cash value, the age of the insured at the time the original policy is terminated, and the company's premium rate for paid-up insurance at the present age of the insured. The amounts of paid-up insurance available at various points in the life of the policy are shown in the table of nonforfeiture values. For example, in a $100,000 straight life policy issued to a man aged 35, the cash value at the end of the tenth year might be $12,000, and the amount of paid-up insurance bought by the cash value might be $36,000.

As in the case of the paid-up additions dividend option discussed in Chapter 9, it is difficult to generalize about whether the insurance available under the paid-up insurance nonforfeiture option is favorably priced. The insurance under the option is available without evidence of insurability, because the exercise of the option reduces the amount of protection. If the insured can provide satisfactory evidence of insurability, the insurance available under the option should be compared with single-premium life insurance available in the market.

The other nonforfeiture option is extended term insurance. Here the policyowner uses the cash value as a single premium to buy a paid-up term policy with a death benefit equal to the death benefit of the original policy. The length of the term is determined by the amount of the cash value, the age of the insured at the time the original policy is terminated, and the company's premium rate for extended term insurance at the present age of the insured. The lengths of the term coverage available at various points in the life of the original policy are shown in the table of nonforfeiture values.

For example, at the end of the tenth year of the above mentioned $100,000 straight life policy, the cash value was $12,000, and the length of the extended term insurance purchased by the cash value might be 24 years plus 182 days. Thus, if the policyowner elects the extended term insurance at the end of the tenth year, the full $100,000 death benefit will be paid to the beneficiary if the insured dies at any time during the next 24½ years. If the insured survives that period, the extended term insurance will expire without any cash value.

The price of extended term insurance is difficult to assess, because single-premium term insurance is not widely available in the market. Even if it were, it probably would not be offered for the odd periods of time associated with the extended term insurance option. As with the other nonforfeiture options, the extended term insurance is available without evidence of insurability.

One cautious generalization can be made about the price of extended term insurance. Because the full death benefit of the original policy can be continued without evidence of insurability and without any further premium payments, the companies expect adverse selection. In other words, they expect that extended term insureds will be in poorer health, on the average, than other insureds. As a consequence, the companies build into the price of extended term insurance a provision for death rates that are higher than normal. It may be generalized, therefore, that the price of extended term insurance tends to be higher than the price of term insurance available in the market.

In most straight life policies currently issued, the extended term insurance option is the one that becomes effective automatically if the policyowner fails to pay a premium by the end of the grace period, allows the policy to lapse, and fails to elect one of the other options. However, if the automatic premium loan clause is operative, the policy will not lapse, and the extended term insurance option will not go into effect.

When a policy with a loan outstanding goes on extended term, the death benefit of the extended term insurance is reduced by the amount of the loan. Furthermore, the cash value used in determining the length of the extended term coverage is also reduced by the amount of the loan.

For example, consider the previously mentioned $100,000 straight life policy issued at age 35, with its cash value of $12,000 at the end of the tenth year. Assume the policy has a $5,000 loan outstanding at the end of the tenth year, when the policyowner elects the extended term insurance option. The $100,000 death benefit is reduced by $5,000, and the $12,000 cash value is reduced by $5,000. The remaining cash value of $7,000 is used as a single premium to buy $95,000 of extended term insurance. The extended term coverage is shortened by the loan, because the original cash value of $12,000 would have extended $100,000 of coverage longer than the remaining cash value of $7,000 will extend $95,000 of coverage.

Settlement Options

The settlement options that are available to the beneficiary were discussed in Chapter 9. In cash-value policies, the same settlement options generally are available to the policyowner for cash values. For example, a policyowner who discontinues premium payments can receive the cash value in installments under the fixed amount or fixed period option. Or the policyowner can leave the cash value under the interest option with full or limited withdrawal privileges. The policyowner at or near retirement age may want to receive the cash value in installments under one of the life annuity options. The various considerations mentioned earlier regarding the beneficiary apply with equal force to the policyowner who wants the cash value paid under the settlement options.

Change of Plan

Many straight life policies contain a change-of-plan provision under which the policy may be converted to a higher-premium plan of insurance, such as a limited-payment life or endowment policy, as of the issue date of the straight life policy. The financial adjustment required for the change varies among companies. One approach, for example, requires the policyowner to pay an amount equal to the difference between the cash values of the two plans, plus a carrying charge of 3 percent of the difference. Because the increased savings component reduces the amount of life insurance protection, the change requires no evidence of insurability.

Conversely, higher-premium plans of insurance usually can be converted to a lower-premium plan, such as straight life, as of the issue date of the higher-premium policy. Here the common practice is for the insurance company to pay the policyowner the difference between the cash values of the two plans. Because the reduction in the savings component increases the amount of life insurance protection, companies require evidence of insurability to make the change.

Chapter 12

How to Select
a Life Insurance
Agent

One of the most important decisions you will ever make in connection
with your life insurance is your choice of an agent. The purpose of
this chapter is to provide you with some suggestions on how to make
the choice a good one.

Why Agents Exist

Most of the life insurance protection that has been sold to individuals through the private sector in the United States has been sold by life insurance agents. You may hear frequently about insurance sold in other ways, such as by direct mail, over the counter in banks, or through advertisements in the major media, but most of the life insurance has been sold by agents dealing directly with customers.

There are at least four reasons why most of the life insurance has been sold by agents. First, the subject matter is distasteful. You probably do not enjoy discussing death and related topics. Thus there is a strong tendency to postpone discussion of life insurance—sometimes until it is too late. Salesmanship may be needed just to get you thinking about life insurance.

Second, life insurance is a financial service under which the insurance company promises to deliver money at some future date. The delivery may be a payment to your family upon your death or, in the case of cash-value life insurance, a payment to you when you surrender the policy or borrow against it. In any case, life insurance requires you to forgo the present enjoyment of the goods and services money will buy in exchange for a promise to deliver money at some unknown future date. You may recognize that you need to buy life insurance, but it may take salesmanship to persuade you to avoid procrastination.

Third, the life insurance policy is a complex financial instrument. Thus a knowledgeable agent can help you select and use your life insurance effectively.

Fourth, agents have political influence. Some of them serve in state legislatures, and their prominence in local communities is a source of grassroots strength. At the national level, agents contribute to LUPAC (the Life Underwriters Political Action Committee), one of the largest political action committees. Over the years, agents' organizations have been at least partially successful in persuading lawmakers to enact and retain restrictions that make it difficult to market life insurance other than through agents.

The Agent's Functions

The preceding discussion suggests some of the functions that are performed by agents. To be more specific, here is a detailed list:

- Persuade you to recognize and discuss the financial problems associated with your death.
- Help you evaluate your life insurance needs.
- Give you sound recommendations in the light of your financial circumstances and objectives.
- Persuade you to buy *now* the life insurance protection you need.
- Keep in touch with you so that your life insurance program will be brought up to date frequently.
- Assist you and your family in using life insurance effectively.

The performance of these functions requires both dedication and competence on the part of the agent. The dedication is needed because life insurance companies generally put the emphasis on selling new policies rather than on servicing existing policies. The agent may receive a commission of 55 percent of the first year's premium (the range is from about 30 percent to more than 100 percent) and commissions of 5 percent on premiums paid after the first year of the policy (the range is from 2 percent to more than 10 percent).

Thus the agent has a financial incentive to spend most of his or her time selling new policies rather than servicing existing policies. You should keep this in mind. If your agent gives you good service, you should do what you can to reward your agent by giving him or her all of your own life insurance business and by recommending your agent to your friends and relatives.

Competence on the part of the agent is needed because of the complexity of life insurance. You cannot rely on the licensing procedures in the various states, because the examinations require only a minimum of knowledge. Nor can you rely upon the training programs of most life insurance companies, because they generally emphasize sales techniques rather than technical knowledge.

Agents may try to impress you with a veritable alphabet soup of organizations, sales achievements, certificates, and designations. Here are just a few of them: CLU, ChFC, CFP, CIC, FIC, RHU, MDRT, AALU, NALU, CEBS, NQA, WLRT, GAMC, LUTCF, FLMI, and ASPA. No useful purpose would be served by an attempt to explain all these abbreviations.

The most rigorous educational experience available to life insurance agents is the Chartered Life Underwriter (CLU) program administered nationally by The American College, an accredited collegiate educational institution located in Bryn Mawr, Pennsylvania.

The study program includes not only technical material on life insurance but also material on many related areas, such as finance, accounting, taxation, business law, and economics. Those who complete the program successfully are awarded the CLU designation and are eligible for membership in the American Society of CLU. Possession of the CLU designation indicates that the holder has passed a series of examinations, met a three-year experience requirement, and taken the following pledge:

> In all my professional relationships, I pledge myself to the following rule of ethical conduct: I shall, in light of all conditions surrounding those I serve, which I shall make every conscientious effort to ascertain and understand, render that service which, in the same circumstances, I would apply to myself.

Even if the agent has received the CLU designation, you cannot be certain what kind of person you are dealing with. The holder of the designation, however, has demonstrated a willingness to undertake and carry to completion a voluntary course of study, and the experience requirement assures that he or she is no newcomer to the life insurance business. It is unlikely that a person would invest the time, effort, and money necessary to acquire the CLU designation unless he or she is serious about a career in the life insurance business.

The Selection Process

A competent and dedicated agent is worth more to you than he or she costs you. On the other hand, an incompetent or unscrupulous agent is worth little or nothing and may have a negative value to you. The objective, then, is to select a competent and dedicated agent.

The most important point is that you must take the initiative and seek out your agent. If you wait to be called upon, your chances of being served by a competent and dedicated agent are significantly reduced. The best agents generally deal with individuals of substantial wealth and income. One can hardly blame the agent, because these clients need and are able to buy large amounts of life insurance, which in turn yield substantial compensation for the agent's efforts.

Another important point is that the adage "you get what you pay for" generally does not apply to the services of a life insurance agent. The best agents tend to work for the best companies—those that are financially strong and offer low-priced policies containing favorable provisions. Further, the commission rates paid to their agents by the best companies frequently are lower than those paid by other companies. The latter companies often pay high commission rates to attract agents, and those rates are reflected in the price of the insurance offered by these companies.

Still another important point is that all the agents of a given insurance company offer the same policies at the same prices. Thus you pay the same price irrespective of the qualifications of the agent who is serving you. Under these circumstances, you should attempt to do business with the best-qualified agent you can find.

The first step in the selection process is to make a list of prospective agents. You may ask those friends and relatives whose judgment you respect for the names of the life insurance agents they regard as the best in the community. Similarly, you may ask your attorney, accountant, or banker for suggestions, emphasizing that competence is the criterion, rather than friendships or other loyalties.

The next step is to become acquainted with the agents you have identified. To assist you in channeling the discussion in a productive way, a series of questions you might ask each prospective agent follows below. You may even insist that the agent provide responses to you in writing.

(1) Are you a full-time life insurance agent?
(2) For how many years have you been a full-time life insurance agent?
(3) What life insurance company or companies do you represent?
(4) If you represent two or more companies, which one is your primary company?
(5) What are your views on placing business with a company other than your primary company?
(6) Do you possess the CLU designation?
(7) If your answer to question 6 is no, how many parts of the CLU study program have you completed successfully, and when was the last one completed?
(8) What schools or conferences do you attend to keep informed about developments in the life insurance business?
(9) What insurance periodicals do you read regularly to keep informed about developments in the life insurance business?
(10) When you prepare an insurance proposal for a client or prospective client, do you allow that person to keep the proposal?
(11) Would you be willing to disclose to me the compensation you receive for making a sale to me, if I should ask you for that information?
(12) Would you be willing to rebate to me a portion of the commission you

receive for making a sale to me, if I should ask you for a rebate?

(13) What procedure do you follow to keep the life insurance programs of your clients up to date?

(14) What arrangements have you made for the servicing of your clients if you die, become disabled, retire, take another position in the business, leave the business, or move to a distant location?

(15) Do you have some testimonial letters from clients who are willing to recommend you?

The following paragraphs contain brief comments about each of the preceding questions.

(1) You should deal with an agent who works full time in the life insurance business, or at least full time in the insurance business. Do not entrust your life insurance affairs to a part-time agent.

(2) You should deal with an agent who has some experience in the business. Seek out an agent who has been in the business full time for at least three years.

(3) You can tell a great deal about an agent by the quality of the companies he or she represents. In view of the discussion in Chapter 7, you may want to deal with an agent of a company which has received top ratings from the A. M. Best Company for ten consecutive years.

(4) The agent who represents primarily one company should be willing to disclose its identity. But the agent may represent several companies and may not have a primary company. Do not select an agent on the basis of whether he or she has a primary company.

(5) Some companies prohibit or discourage their agents from placing business with other companies, even when placing the business elsewhere is in the buyer's best interest. It is important for you to have the agent discuss his or her views on this matter.

(6) The CLU designation is discussed earlier in this chapter.

(7) The CLU program currently consists of ten examinations. Be wary if the agent has not successfully passed at least some of the examinations in recent years.

(8) Participation in continuing education programs may be an indication of the agent's sophistication in insurance matters.

(9) Some of the important insurance periodicals are the *National Underwriter* (a weekly newspaper), *Best's Review* (a monthly magazine), the *CLU Journal* (the quarterly journal of the American Society of CLU), *Life Association News* (the monthly magazine of the National

Association of Life Underwriters), *Life Insurance Selling* (a monthly magazine), *The Insurance Forum* (a four-page monthly periodical), and *Probe* (a four-page periodical published twenty-two times per year).

(10) Be wary of an agent who does not allow you to keep a proposal he or she has prepared to show your insurance needs and the agent's recommendations.

(11) Some agents are influenced primarily by the interests of their clients, and some agents are influenced primarily by their own interests. You may or may not want to ask an agent to disclose the commission he or she receives from making a sale to you, but be wary of an agent who will not disclose the information if you request it.

(12) State insurance laws invariably prohibit agents from giving rebates, and some of these laws also prohibit consumers from receiving rebates. Antirebating laws are anticompetitive and a result of the political influence of insurance agents. But until such laws are repealed, rebates are illegal. Do not deal with an agent who offers you a rebate of any kind, or who would give you one if you asked for it.

(13) The agent should be able to describe how he or she will help you keep your insurance program up to date.

(14) If your agent is no longer able to serve you, another agent will have to be selected. The plans that an agent has made to deal with this contingency may provide you with important information about how the agent operates.

(15) If the agent has some satisfied clients, they should be willing to provide testimonial letters.

In the end, your selection of an agent will be based on your subjective assessment of his or her honesty, competence, and integrity. Discussion of the questions listed in this chapter will provide you with information and assistance in making that assessment.

Chapter 13

Buying Life Insurance Without an Agent

As indicated in Chapter 12, most of the life insurance protection sold through the private sector in the United States has been sold through the efforts of life insurance agents. It is possible, however, to buy life insurance without an agent. Some such sources of life insurance are discussed in this chapter.

Non-Agency Organizations

Some organizations market life insurance without using the services of life insurance agents. For purposes of discussion, these organizations may be divided into three categories: (1) savings banks, (2) organizations that specialize in selling life insurance to designated groups, and (3) "direct response" marketers.

Savings Bank Life Insurance

Life insurance is offered over the counter in mutual savings banks in three states—Massachusetts, New York, and Connecticut. To be eligible for savings bank life insurance (SBLI), a person must be either residing or working regularly in the particular state when the policy is purchased. The amount that may be purchased is limited by SBLI laws.

Massachusetts SBLI, the oldest of the three, was established by an act of the Massachusetts legislature in 1907. The current limit on the amount of life insurance that may be issued to an individual is $1,000 times the number of issuing banks in the state. As of November 1, 1983, there were 62 issuing banks, so the limit was $62,000 of life insurance for an individual. An additional 92 banks in the state were participating as agency banks, which may accept applications and premium payments as agents of an issuing bank.

New York SBLI was established in 1939. The amount that may be issued to one individual is $30,000, with some exceptions. As of December 31, 1983, there were 51 issuing banks and 41 agency banks in the New York SBLI system.

Connecticut SBLI was established in 1941. The amount of life insurance that may be issued to one individual is $25,000. At the end of 1983, 54 banks in the state were offering SBLI.

Although the SBLI programs in Massachusetts, New York, and Connecticut have been successful, no other states have enacted similar legislation. The reason is simple—the political influence of life insurance agents has prevented the establishment of SBLI systems in other states. The agents' influence may be illustrated by an incident that occurred in 1967, when an unsuccessful attempt was made to increase the limit in the Connecticut SBLI system from $5,000 to $15,000. The following excerpt from a newspaper story gives some of the flavor of the agents' opposition to SBLI:*

> Insurance men Thursday gave the Capitol its biggest and noisiest hearing of this legislative session.

---

*Ivan Robinson, "Insurance Opposition Vocal at Hearing on Bank Ceiling," *Hartford Times*, April 14, 1967.

About 500 of them showed up at a Banking Committee hearing to oppose a bill that would raise the ceiling on savings bank life insurance from the present $5,000 to $15,000.

They filled every seat in the Hall of the House and its gallery and stood as many as 10 deep in the aisles. And they cheered, applauded, booed, hissed and catcalled during testimony.

Attorney George Ritter, Hartford's deputy mayor, got the brunt of the hazing when he spoke out in favor of eliminating ceilings altogether on bank insurance.

Specializing Organizations

A number of organizations specialize in selling life insurance to individuals in designated categories. Some of these organizations use no agents, although some of them sell some of their insurance through agents. A few of these organizations are described briefly in the following paragraphs.

The Teachers Insurance and Annuity Association of America (TIAA), together with its companion organization, the College Retirement Equities Fund, provides retirement plans for persons employed by colleges, universities, and certain other nonprofit educational institutions. In addition, TIAA offers individual life insurance to such persons and their spouses. TIAA handles its life insurance operations by mail, and employs salaried representatives who are available by telephone at its New York City headquarters.

The USAA Life Insurance Company, a subsidiary of the United Services Automobile Association, has specialized over the years in selling life insurance to present and former members of the military. Insurance is sold and serviced primarily by mail and over the telephone from the company's San Antonio headquarters.

Ministers Life—A Mutual Life Insurance Company specializes in selling life insurance to individuals in church-related professions. For many years the company handled its business by mail, but in recent years it began transacting business through agents as well. Insurance is also sold through salaried employees directed from the company's Minneapolis headquarters.

Direct Response Marketers

Some companies sell life insurance through "direct response" methods. This phrase encompasses such techniques as direct mail, television advertisements with toll-free numbers, and newspaper and magazine advertisements that include application forms.

Direct response marketing of life insurance has several distinguishing characteristics. First, companies often use celebrities, such as entertainers, former athletes, or former politicians, who extol the virtues of the insurance being offered.

Second, the death benefit offered is often small—in many instances, less than $2,000. Furthermore, the death benefit in the first one or two years may be even smaller—often no more than a return of the premiums. Sometimes the coverage is described as "supplemental," presumably to suggest that the coverage is not a substitute for adequate life insurance purchased through other means.

Third, companies sometimes offer the insurance "with no questions asked," but fail to disclose that the insurance is expensive for buyers in good health because it is expected that many of those applying for the insurance will be in poor health. The lack of disclosure often is accomplished by emphasizing a premium of, say, "only $6.95 a month," without mentioning the small amount of life insurance purchased by that premium.

Fourth, heavy emphasis frequently is placed on policy provisions that are common to life insurance policies. For example, the fact that the premiums do not increase and the fact that the policy builds cash values sometimes are mentioned as though they are unique features of the coverage being offered.

Fifth, direct response sales presentations often emphasize that no agent will call, thus implying that the absence of an agent is necessarily desirable. This feature of direct response selling is perhaps the most obnoxious from the point of view of life insurance agents, and may explain more than any other feature why agents find direct response methods distasteful.

If you decide to investigate the possibility of purchasing some life insurance from a direct response marketer, follow the procedures suggested in earlier chapters for measuring the amount of life insurance you need, determining an appropriate type of life insurance for your situation, and selecting a life insurance company. If you follow the suggested procedures, and if you are in reasonably good health for your age, it is unlikely that you will purchase your life insurance from a direct response marketer.

Government Agencies

Outside the private sector, life insurance may be available to you through various government agencies. Among these are the Social

Security Administration, the Veterans' Administration, and the Wisconsin State Life Fund.

Social Security

Nearly all Americans employed full time are covered by Social Security. The program provides substantial life insurance benefits—under the name "survivors' benefits"—particularly when the covered worker has young children. The level of these survivors' benefits makes Social Security an important part of the typical worker's life insurance program. Examples of these benefits, together with suggestions on how to obtain information on the Social Security benefits for which you are eligible, are found in Chapter 2.

Veterans' Administration

Armed services personnel and veterans have long enjoyed some form of government-subsidized life insurance as one of the perquisites for military service to the United States. Over the years, however, many of the details of such coverages and their administrative procedures have been changed. For several decades, the Veterans' Administration has been involved in one way or another in many of these programs.

The coverages offered to military personnel and veterans of World Wars I and II were optional. The coverage for persons in military service during the Korean War was mandatory, but was provided by the government without cost to the individual. Coverage after discharge from military service was optional. In recent years, coverage for military personnel has again been made optional, and has been offered through a cooperative venture involving the Veterans' Administration and the life insurance industry.

As a general rule, the coverages offered to military personnel and to veterans through the Veterans' Administration have been favorable for the insured. In recent years, however, for the veteran to continue the coverage, it has been necessary for the insurance to be converted to a regular policy issued by a commercial company. The fact that the conversion can be accomplished without evidence of insurability makes the transaction simple, but it is important for the insured to be cautious in selecting the company for conversion.

Furthermore, the conversion process may limit the insured as to the type of life insurance that may be obtained. For that reason, the veteran who can qualify for life insurance probably should forget about the conversion privilege and buy life insurance in accordance with the procedures described in this book.

Wisconsin State Life Fund

The Wisconsin State Life fund is a state-operated organization that offers individual life insurance to persons in Wisconsin at the time the insurance is purchased. Its operations are handled by mail, and only limited amounts of life insurance are available. Information about the Fund may be obtained by writing to the Wisconsin insurance department at the address shown in Appendix C.

Group Life Insurance

This book deals primarily with individual life insurance—that is, life insurance purchased by individuals—in contrast to group life insurance. The most common form of group life insurance is purchased by an employer to cover employees. In this section, several forms of group life insurance are discussed.

Employer Group Life

Virtually all large employers and many small employers offer some form of group life insurance to their employees. In terms of premium payments, group life insurance plans are either noncontributory or contributory.

A noncontributory group life plan is one in which the employees pay nothing. The cost of the plan is borne by the employer. If you are an eligible employee, you are automatically covered in a noncontributory plan.

A contributory group life plan is one in which the employees pay a portion of the cost. The remainder of the cost is borne by the employer. Most contributory plans provide that eligible employees may enroll or refrain from enrolling. If an employee wants the coverage without evidence of insurability, however, he or she usually must enroll when first eligible or during some later special enrollment period announced by the employer.

Most group life plans consist of one-year renewable term insurance. The insurance company calculates the employer's premium on the basis of amounts of insurance and ages of the covered employees. However, the employees in many contributory plans pay a flat amount per month per $1,000 of coverage regardless of age. Some employers charge 60 cents (more in the case of hazardous occupations), but many employers charge less.

The effect of the flat rate is that older employees receive a bargain. Younger employees sometimes pay as much as they would to obtain individual one-year renewable term coverage, or perhaps even more. However, the flat contribution rate means that the price looks increasingly attractive to younger employees as they get older.

Perhaps the best way to view such a plan is that older employees receive a subsidy from the employer, while younger employees pay their own way. Only very young employees are overcharged relative to market prices, and even in such instances the amount of the overcharge usually is not enough to be concerned about.

An important aspect of group life insurance is the conversion privilege. If your coverage terminates because you leave your employer or retire, you may obtain individual coverage from the insurance company in which the group plan is in force. You must exercise your conversion privilege within thirty days of the termination of your employment, and you must pay the premium rate associated with your age at the time of conversion. However, you can obtain the individual insurance without evidence of insurability. You should check your conversion privilege so that you will know what to expect when your coverage terminates.

Some group life plans are written on a cash-value basis. These are relatively rare, however, and are beyond the scope of this discussion.

You should enroll for the group life coverage made available by your employer. As a general rule, such coverage is reasonably priced for the employee.

Association Group Life

Many professional associations and other organizations make life insurance available to their members. Such coverage has some characteristics of individual life insurance and some characteristics of group life insurance.

Association group life coverage usually is term insurance. Premium rates are based on age and usually increase periodically as the individual grows older. The cost of the coverage is borne entirely by the member, who receives premium notices directly from the insurance company or from the administrator of the program. Often the member must show evidence of insurability to qualify for coverage, although the requirements usually are less strict than for individual life insurance. The amounts of insurance available are limited.

Sometimes the insurance company pays the association a flat percentage of the premiums paid by the members. In other cases, the association is paid either dividends or some other form of compensation. As a general rule, therefore, the purchase of group coverage by a member is a method for making a contribution to the association.

Partly because the member pays the entire cost, association group life usually is more expensive than employer group life, in which at least some of the cost is borne by the employer. The coverage may be less expensive than individual term life insurance available in the open market, but you should not assume this is the case; sometimes you can buy individual coverage at a lower price.

Association group life coverage is not as flexible or as reliable as a good one-year renewable term policy issued on an individual basis. Often the coverage can be continued only if you remain a member of the association. The coverage can be terminated by the association or by the insurance company. Unlike individual term policies, association group coverage may not be convertible. (The conversion privilege in individual term policies is discussed in Chapter 10.)

Association group life coverage is worth considering if you are a member of an organization that offers such coverage and if you intend to remain a member for a long period of time. Before enrolling, however, check the cost and the terms of the coverage. Even then, if you decide to buy, do not rely heavily upon association group coverage as a part of your life insurance program, because the coverage may be terminated for reasons beyond your control.

Credit Life

Many lending institutions have arranged for insurance on the lives of their borrowers. Usually this coverage, called credit life insurance, is on a group basis and provides that any remaining indebtedness is cancelled at the death of the borrower.

In some instances credit life insurance is included automatically in loan transactions "without any specific extra charge." The insurance written through many credit unions is an example.

In most instances, however, credit life insurance is optional with the borrower, and he or she pays a specific premium for the coverage. Some serious problems are found with this form of insurance.

First, the premium is designed so that the borrowers as a group will pay more than the cost of the coverage. The excess is then returned to the lender by the insurance company as a dividend or commission. (In some instances the insurance company is affiliated with the lending institution.) Therefore, credit life insurance is likely to be more expensive than employer group life, in which the employer pays at least some of the cost.

Second, the general nature of credit life insurance has led to a phenomenon called "reverse competition." When insurance companies bid for the credit life insurance business of a lending institution, frequently the focus is upon the size of the dividend or commission to the lender, rather than upon the premium. The lender tends to buy the coverage from the insurance company that offers the largest dividend or commission, rather than from the insurance company that offers the lowest premium to the borrower. Since the insurance company offering the largest dividend or commission is likely to be the one that charges the highest premium, the effect of the competition is to increase the cost of the coverage to the borrower—hence the phrase "reverse competition."

Third, although the coverage is optional, borrowers often think the coverage is mandatory. Thus, they often buy the coverage without knowing how its cost compares with other forms of insurance.

These problem areas are well known in the insurance business, and credit life insurance rates are subject to regulation by some state insurance departments. As in other areas, however, regulation is uneven and spotty.

The problems described above do not exist when credit life insurance is included automatically in loan transactions "without any specific extra charge." The cost is borne by the lender, who has an incentive to buy it at the lowest possible cost.

When credit life insurance is optional and paid for by the borrower, it sometimes should be considered despite the problems. Because credit life usually is available without evidence of insurability, it should be considered by anyone with insurability problems. And because credit life premium rates often are the same irrespective of age, it should be considered by borrowers beyond, say, the age of 50.

The net effect of optional credit life, however, is to increase the effective rate of interest charged by the lender. If you are in good health, you should include provision for debts in determining your life insurance needs, as suggested in Chapter 2, and decline to buy credit life insurance when you borrow.

Chapter 14

The Life Insurance Purchase

Earlier chapters have dealt with questions of how much to buy, what kind to buy, what company to choose, and what the policy language is all about. This chapter deals with several miscellaneous topics that should be considered as you consummate your purchase of a life insurance policy.

Completing the Application

The application for life insurance usually consists of two parts. The first part requires such information as your address, your date of birth, the amount and kind of insurance you want, the premium, the beneficiary designation, whether you want the automatic premium loan clause to be in effect, and so on. This type of information is needed by the company to prepare the policy.

The second part of the application requires information about your health, habits, and occupation, on the basis of which the insurance company decides whether it is willing to write the insurance. Sometimes the second part of the application is completed by a physician or paramedic in the course of a medical examination. An examination usually is required when the amount of insurance applied for is large, when you are beyond a specified age, or when your medical history is complex. Companies differ in their rules about these items—such as what constitutes a "large" amount of insurance and what age limit applies.

In many applications, however, the second part is completed by an agent, in which case it is called a "nonmedical application." Here the agent asks a series of medical questions and records the answers. Most companies use the nonmedical application when the amount of insurance requested is less than a specified figure, when the proposed insured is below a specified age, and when the medical history is acceptable. The company will require a medical examination if it is not satisfied with the results of the nonmedical application. The reason for the nonmedical approach is that the companies save more money by eliminating the medical examination than they lose in additional death claims.

The insurance company has other sources of information about you. Sometimes the company will request an investigation by a credit-reporting organization such as Equifax. The report the insurance company receives may be based in part on information about you that the inspection company has in its files from previous investigations and in part on information obtained in a new investigation. This is why you may sometimes hear from friends, neighbors, or business colleagues that someone has been asking questions about you.

Another source of information is the Medical Information Bureau (MIB), which is an information clearinghouse operated by a large number of insurance companies on a cooperative basis. It is sometimes said that the insurance companies are "ganging up" on individual applicants. The insurance companies argue, however, that such a clearinghouse is needed because of the substantial number of applicants who submit fraudulent information in an attempt to obtain insurance coverage. The companies argue that the MIB helps protect them from such applicants, thereby keeping the price of insurance reasonable for applicants who are acting in good faith.

Read the application before you sign it. Usually the agent will fill out the form, but you should verify what has been written there. Also, when you read the form, you will see what kind of authorizations you are signing, and you will see various disclosures about the type of information the insurance company will be assembling in connection with your application.

When you apply for insurance, tell the company the truth about yourself. Beware of the agent who advises you to play fast and loose on the application. For example, when you mention some illness in response to a question on the application, the agent might say, "Well, the company really isn't interested in that, so let's leave it out."

If your agent is the type of person who encourages a few little falsehoods on the application, he or she probably is the type of person who tells you a few little falsehoods about the insurance you are buying. Do not deal with such an agent; if you insist on doing so, you deserve the aggravation the future probably holds for you and your family. You should avoid acquiring a reputation as a person who lies to insurance companies. It is important to have the life insurance you need, but it is not worth turning yourself into a dishonest person to get it.

The First Premium

Life insurance can be put into effect in two ways. One is to complete the two parts of the application, wait for the company to approve the insurance, and then pay the first premium upon delivery of the policy. When this procedure is followed, the insurance does not take effect until the policy has been delivered and the first premium has been paid. The result can be disastrous. You might change to a more hazardous occupation between the date of application and the date of policy delivery. You might develop some health problem during the interval. Or you might even die. If there is any significant change in your health, habits, or occupation between the date of application and the date of policy delivery, the agent must withhold delivery and notify the insurance company of the changed circumstances.

The other approach is preferable because it avoids these possible complications. The two parts of the application are completed and the first premium is sent to the insurance company with the application. When this procedure is followed, the insurance, if approved by the company exactly as applied for, takes effect on the last of three dates: the date the first part of the application is completed, the date the second part of the application is completed, and the date the check is written. If the application is declined by the company, the money is refunded to the applicant. If the company offers the coverage but at a premium higher than that applied for, the applicant has the choice of a refund or paying the balance of the first premium upon delivery of the policy. In the latter case, the insurance takes effect at the time of delivery and payment of the balance.

When the first premium accompanies the application, the insurance company considers the proposed insured in terms of the circumstances at the time of application. If the proposed insured is acceptable, the insurance takes effect at the time of application. There are cases on record in which the proposed insured died in an accident almost immediately after completing the application, so that the death claim went in with the application. In this type of situation, if the proposed insured is acceptable at the time of the application and a check is sent with the application, the company will pay the death benefit to the beneficiary.

When you decide to buy the insurance, arrange to have it effective at the earliest possible moment. In some companies, it is necessary to send in the full amount of the first premium with the application to bind the coverage. In other companies, however, it is possible to bind the coverage by sending in a portion of the first premium, with the balance of the first premium payable upon delivery of the policy.

The only disadvantage of sending in the first premium with the application is that you pay the first premium before you see the policy. However, most policies issued today include a "free look" provision, under which you are permitted to return the policy for a full refund within, say, ten days after policy delivery. Also, it should be possible for you to examine a sample policy. Any company worthy of your patronage makes sample policies available to its agents. If the agent does not have or cannot quickly obtain a sample policy, find another agent.

Quantity Discounts

Years ago, life insurance companies usually charged the same premium rate per $1,000 of death benefit regardless of the size of the policy. Today, however, most companies charge lower premium rates on large policies than on otherwise comparable small policies. Thus life insurance involves "quantity discounts."

Companies may differentiate by size of policy in at least three ways. One is to offer different policies in various size ranges. For example, a company may offer an endowment at age 90 if the death benefit is under $50,000, and a life paid up at age 95 policy if the death benefit is $50,000 or more.

A second approach is to offer the same policy regardless of size but to charge different premium rates in various size ranges. For example, under this "band" approach, a company may charge a premium rate of $20 per $1,000 of death benefit (for some type of policy at some particular age) if the death benefit is in the $2,000 to $4,999 range, $18 in the $5,000 to $9,999 range, $17 in the $10,000 to $24,999 range, and $16.50 if the death benefit is $25,000 or more.

A third approach, which is the most common today, is to offer the same policy regardless of size but to charge different premium rates for every policy size. This procedure is accomplished by establishing a "basic" premium rate and an annual "policy fee." To determine the premium for a policy, the basic rate is multiplied by the number of thousands of death benefit, and then the policy fee is added. For example, a company may have a basic premium rate of $16 per $1,000 of death benefit (for some type of policy at some age), and an annual policy fee of $15. In this case, the premium for a $5,000 policy is $95 ($16 multiplied by 5, plus $15), or $19 per $1,000 of death benefit. At $10,000, the premium rate is $17.50 per $1,000 of death benefit; at $25,000, the premium rate is $16.60; at $50,000, the premium rate is $16.30; and so on.

· Quantity discounts are of considerable significance if you are contemplating the purchase of a small policy, but are of little significance if you are buying a large policy. To illustrate, a policy fee of $15 adds $3 to the premium rate per $1,000 of death benefit for a $5,000 policy, but adds only 15 cents to the premium rate for a $100,000 policy.

Nonsmoker Discounts

Years ago, life insurance companies invariably charged the same premium rate per $1,000 of death benefit whether the insured was a smoker or not. In recent years, however, evidence has been accumulating rapidly that there are substantial differences in mortality rates between smokers and nonsmokers. Today, therefore, many companies charge lower rates for nonsmokers than for smokers. If you are a nonsmoker, be sure to inquire about nonsmoker discounts.

A few companies are going beyond smoking habits and offering discounts for individuals who keep in shape by jogging or by other regular exercise activities. If you follow a regular program of exercise, inquire about whether the company you are considering offers such discounts.

Do not be taken in, however, by companies that offer discount programs in an effort to conceal overpriced offerings. Some companies heavily emphasize discounts in their sales materials, but even with the discounts their insurance is high-priced. "We give a 20 percent discount to joggers" is of little value to the consumer if the price before the discount is so high that the price after the discount is still above the price charged by reputable companies that do not offer the discount. Be sure to follow the procedure discussed in earlier chapters on how to select a company.

Insurability Problems

Most individuals qualify for "standard" coverage. This means they pay the regular premium rates charged by the company. Some individuals, however, qualify for "substandard" insurance (sometimes called "special class" insurance), which means they pay premium rates that are higher than the company's standard rates. The reason for the higher rates is that the person's characteristics suggest he or she is a member of a group likely to experience higher mortality rates than are found among standard insureds. Among such characteristics might be a health impairment or a hazardous occupation.

Substandard categories are many. Some involve premiums only slightly higher than standard, while others involve premiums substantially higher than standard. And then, some applicants have problems so acute that they cannot qualify for life insurance.

Suppose you have an insurability problem, which causes you to be offered either substandard coverage or no coverage. In that case, consult a competent agent, who should be familiar with the practices of various companies with respect to insurability problems. Companies differ substantially in this area. Some do better than others with diabetes; some do better than others with heart problems; and so on.

Do not be taken in by claims of liberal treatment. Remember that companies differ widely in terms of price for standard coverage. Since companies differ widely in terms of liberality on substandard coverage, the result is a completely unpredictable market for a person with an insurability problem.

Consider the case of Betty, who is aged 52 and overweight. She wanted life insurance. Knowing she probably would qualify only for substandard insurance among the major companies, her agent tried a small company that was reputed to be liberal with persons who are overweight. Back came a policy labeled on the front as "standard" insurance. Upon examination, however, the agent discovered that the company's "standard" insurance was higher in price than the category of "substandard" insurance for which Betty would qualify in a major company. The moral of the story is that the superficially attractive offer may not be so attractive under scrutiny.

Fractional Premiums

The simplest way to handle the premiums on a life insurance policy is to pay them annually (once each year). Many policyowners, however, prefer to divide the premiums into smaller amounts and pay them more frequently. Instead of annually, premiums usually may be paid semiannually, quarterly, or monthly. An exception to this general rule is that companies normally specify a minimum premium, such as $10, that they are willing to handle.

Companies usually impose a "carrying charge" for paying premiums other than annually. Carrying charges are justified because the company loses interest through the delay in receiving premium payments, and because the company incurs additional expenses to collect the larger number of smaller premiums. Companies also argue that they lose money because policyowners are more likely to discontinue their policies when they pay premiums more frequently than annually.

Further, in some cases the carrying charges include a small life insurance component. For example, if the insured dies three months after payment of the first quarterly premium, the company will not collect the other three quarterly premiums for that year. But if the annual premium is paid, and if the company refunds the unearned portion of the premium at the insured's death (as discussed in Chapter 9), three-fourths of the annual premium will be paid to the beneficiary. Therefore, the carrying charges include a life insurance component only in the case of companies that do not refund the unearned portion of the premium at the insured's death.

When a person borrows money, the interest charges cover not only interest but also the expenses associated with collecting the loan payments and a charge to cover loan delinquencies. Therefore, the carrying charges for paying premiums more frequently than annually are analogous to interest charges. In the discussion that follows, the above mentioned small element of life insurance is disregarded.

Because the carrying charges can be substantial, it is important for policyowners to be aware of the costs associated with the payment of fractional premiums. Suppose, for example, that the semiannual premium is 52 percent of the annual premium. Thus, if the annual premium is $100, each of the two semiannual premiums is $52. Since the total of the semiannual payments for the year amounts to $104 in contrast to the annual premium of $100, the arrangement is sometimes described—deceptively—as a 4 percent carrying charge. Such a description is deceptive because the arrangement resembles an annual interest charge of about 16.7 percent.

The latter figure may be deduced readily. If you pay a $52 semiannual premium instead of a $100 annual premium, you defer the payment of $48 for six months. You then pay the $48 six months later, along with a $4 carrying charge. This means you pay $4 for the use of $48 for six months, which is about the same as paying $8 for the use of $48 for one year. Dividing $8 by $48 yields an annual interest rate of about 16.7 percent.

Here again, as in the case of companies that charge interest in advance on policy loans, the companies are failing to disclose the effective interest rate. Until such disclosure is required (and in view of the political power of the insurance industry, it may never be required), it is important that you realize the financial implications of paying premiums other than annually. Some of the common factors applied to annual premiums, and the associated annual percentage rates (to use the terminology of the federal truth-in-lending law), are shown in Table 11.

Another method for determining the annual percentage rate associated with fractional premiums is to use a family of simple formulas. All you need to know is the annual premium and the fractional premium. Then, by plugging those figures into the appropriate for-

Table 11
Fractional Premium Factors and Corresponding Annual Percentage Rates

	Factors	Annual Percentage Rates
Semiannual premium:	.51	8.2%
	.515	12.4
	.52	16.7
Quarterly premium:	.26	10.7%
	.2625	13.4
	.265	16.1
Monthly premium:	.0875	10.8%
	.0883	12.8
	.09	17.2

mula, you can quickly approximate the annual percentage rate. The formulas are as follows:

$$APR = \frac{2(2S - A)}{A - S}$$

$$APR = \frac{12(4Q - A)}{5A - 2Q}$$

$$APR = \frac{36(12M - A)}{13A + 42M}$$

where APR is the annual percentage rate expressed as a decimal, A is the annual premium, S is the semiannual premium, Q is the quarterly premium, and M is the monthly premium.*

To illustrate, suppose the annual premium for the policy you are considering is $1,000, and the quarterly premium is $265. To approximate the annual percentage rate, use the second of the above three formulas. The calculations are as follows:

---

*For a description of the derivation of these formulas, see Joseph M. Belth, "A Note on the Cost of Fractional Premiums," *Journal of Risk and Insurance,* Vol. XLV, No. 4 (December, 1978), pp. 683–687.

$$\text{APR} = \frac{12[4(265) - 1,000]}{5(1,000) - 2(265)} = \frac{12(1,060 - 1,000)}{5,000 - 530}$$

$$= \frac{12(60)}{4,470} = \frac{720}{4,470} = .161 = 16.1\%$$

Frequently you are better off paying premiums annually even if you have to borrow the money to do so. In the first place, the gross cost of borrowing may be less than the carrying charge. In the second place, the interest you pay is deductible for federal income tax purposes (if you itemize your deductions), while the carrying charge is not.

To illustrate this point, suppose your annual premium is $1,000 and your semiannual premium is $520. If you pay semiannually, you incur nondeductible carrying charges of $40. Now suppose you pay $520 toward the annual premium and borrow the remaining $480 for six months. Let's say the annual interest rate you have to pay on the loan is 12 percent. If you pay off the loan six months later, you pay $508.80, including interest. In other words, you have incurred deductible interest of $28.80, rather than nondeductible carrying charges of $40.

The disadvantage of the borrowing approach is that the insurance company does not send you a reminder about repayment of the loan. In the preceding illustration, for example, you would not receive a reminder to pay the $508.80 at the end of six months. On the other hand, if you pay premiums semiannually, you would receive a premium notice each time.

There are at least two additional reasons for finding out the cost of fractional premiums if you contemplate paying premiums other than annually. First, some companies impose carrying charges that are large—in some cases even larger than those shown in Table 11.

Second, sales illustrations invariably are based on annual premiums, and the system described in Chapter 8 is based on annual premiums. Thus it is possible for you to be misled into making a purchase decision based on annual premiums if you contemplate paying premiums other than annually. One company, for example, whose policyowners almost all pay premiums monthly, multiplies the annual premium by .095 to determine the monthly premium. That translates into an annual percentage rate of 29.7 percent.

For the policyowner who wishes to pay premiums monthly, most companies offer an arrangement involving pre-authorized checks. These plans are sometimes called "check-o-matic" or "automatic bank check" plans. Under these plans you authorize the insurance company to draw against your checking account each month. Since the insurance company does not have to send you premium notices, the carrying charges for these plans usually are smaller than the carrying charges for regular monthly premiums. If you want to pay monthly premiums, and if you have no qualms about allowing an insurance company to have access to your checking account, consider a pre-authorized check plan. On the other hand, if you prefer to maintain control over your checking account, do not use a pre-authorized check plan.

Financed Insurance

In these days of "buy now, pay later," it is possible to buy nearly any commodity or service and finance the purchase. Since life insurance itself is an important financial instrument, it is not surprising to find various techniques for financing it. The phrase "financed insurance" refers to any arrangement under which all or part of a life insurance premium is paid by borrowing.

One problem with financed insurance is that the financing scheme sometimes dominates the life insurance discussion. Some agents preach the advantages of financed insurance without carefully considering the amount of insurance needed, the type of insurance that is appropriate, or the underlying price and quality of the policy. An important point to remember about financing, therefore, is that it should be discussed only as a final step in buying life insurance.

The most common form of financed insurance today is often called "minimum deposit" or, for short, "mini-dip." The plan frequently is based on a straight life policy, and each year the policyowner pays just enough to keep the policy in force with a maximum loan against it. Specifically, each year the policyowner pays the annual premium, plus the interest on the accrued policy loan, minus the increase in the policy's loan value. The arrangement transforms a straight life policy (which contains a decreasing protection component and an increasing savings component) into a decreasing term policy with no savings component.*

Years ago, when bank loan interest rates typically were below policy loan interest rates, the corresponding arrangement was called "the bank loan plan." It worked the same way, except that the borrowing was done at a bank through a collateral assignment of the policy, rather than from the insurance company under the loan clause.

Under minimum deposit, as in the case of any policy with a loan outstanding, the amount payable to the beneficiary at the death of the insured is the death benefit minus the loan. To make the arrangement more attractive, most companies offer a dividend option under which enough one-year term insurance is purchased to cover the amount of the loan. (This option was discussed in Chapter 9.) When this option is elected, the amount payable to the beneficiary is level—a result accomplished by superimposing an increasing amount of one-year term insurance on top of a decreasing amount of protection.

Two advantages usually are alleged to be associated with the minimum-deposit plan. The first is that the price of the protection may be lower in a straight life policy than in a term policy. In other words, it is argued that the policyowner who wants only protection and no savings component may save money by buying straight life and using the minimum-deposit plan instead of buying term insurance. This may or may not be true in any given case. Furthermore, it is difficult to generalize in this area because of the complexities of direct price comparisons between markedly different types of policies. You need not concern yourself about this problem if you follow the procedure recommended in Chapter 6 for selecting an appropriate type of policy.

The other alleged advantage of the minimum-deposit plan is in the income tax area. As a general rule, policy loan interest paid is deductible by policyowners who itemize their deductions. At the same time, the inside interest in cash-value life insurance is income-tax-deferred, and eventually is either fully or partially income-tax-exempt. (For a

---

*Some agents get so carried away with their sales pitch that they refer to the plan as a "minimum-deposit policy." Although some policies are designed with minimum deposit in mind, there is no such thing as a minimum-deposit policy. The minimum-deposit arrangement is simply one method by which to pay the premiums on a cash-value life insurance policy.

discussion of this point, see Chapter 5.) The result is a form of tax leverage, with the amount of the leverage dependent upon the policyowner's income tax bracket.

The Internal Revenue Service is aware of the implications of this tax leverage and for many years has been playing a kind of game with the life insurance business. Early in the game some life insurance agents had the idea of selling single-premium life insurance to high-income-tax-bracket policyowners who would borrow the full amount of the single premium. The idea was a bonanza for these policyowners (and earned the agents some large commissions) because the interplay between the tax-deferred inside interest and the tax-deductible loan interest gave the policyowner life insurance protection at a low and often negative net outlay. The IRS response was to have Congress change the rules so that interest on a loan taken out for the purpose of buying single-premium life insurance was no longer deductible.

Undaunted, some agents shifted to the idea of using limited-payment life policies (such as ten-payment life or twenty-payment life), and having their policyowners pay all of the premiums in a single sum. When this is done, the insurance company gives a discount on premiums paid in advance of their due dates, which means that the advance premiums constitute an interest-bearing fund. The policyowner would obtain the single sum by borrowing. Again, the result was a bonanza for high-tax-bracket policyowners (and their agents), because of the interplay between the tax-deferred inside interest and the tax-deductible loan interest. The IRS response was to have Congress change the rules so that interest on a loan taken for the purpose of paying a substantial number of premiums in advance was no longer deductible.*

Still undaunted, some agents turned to the bank loan plan or minimum-deposit plan. The arrangement involves borrowing only a part of each annual premium as it falls due, so there are no large single sum borrowings. Nevertheless, the interplay between the tax-deferred inside interest and the tax-deductible loan interest creates a bonanza for high-tax-bracket policyowners. This time the rules were

---

*In the early days of this arrangement, there was an extra bonanza for the policyowner because the interest on the premiums paid in advance was not taxable, but Congress closed this loophole by making such interest taxable.

changed so that interest on a loan taken as part of a systematic plan of borrowing to pay premiums was no longer deductible. However, the loophole was only partly closed, because the rules provide that an arrangement is not to be construed as systematic borrowing if the policyowner pays in full (without borrowing) at least four of the first seven annual premiums on the policy.

You should understand some of the agent's motivations in recommending the minimum-deposit plan. Suppose you have decided to increase your life insurance protection by $100,000 and do not want to put any more of your savings into life insurance. If the agent sells you a $100,000 one-year renewable term policy, the first-year commission might be about $100. If the agent sells you a $100,000 straight life policy on the minimum-deposit plan, however, the first-year commission might be about $800. This commission differential gives the agent a powerful vested interest in the minimum-deposit approach. These comments are not intended to suggest that the agent necessarily will give you advice contrary to your best interests, but you should appreciate the pressures under which the agent operates. Remember that the agent may have a family to feed, just as you may.

Avoid the minimum-deposit plan and other financing schemes unless three conditions are met. First, the amount of insurance should be substantial and you should be in a substantial tax bracket, so that the tax leverage has a significant value for you. For example, if the amount of cash-value life insurance is less than $50,000 and if you are not in at least a 40 percent tax bracket, the minimum-deposit approach may not be worth your effort.

Second, you should be willing to put up with the complexities of the minimum-deposit plan and be willing to "play the game" with the IRS. This is important because a large and growing interest deduction may attract attention to your income tax return.

Third, you should thoroughly understand the plan, and you should not get heavily involved in a minimum-deposit program without competent legal advice. Some policyowners, following the advice of life insurance agents, have run afoul of the previously mentioned four-out-of-seven rule, thus disqualifying the loan interest as a tax deduction. Furthermore, it is the exception rather than the rule for life insurance agents to point out carefully the potential income-tax problems that can overtake the policyowner many years down the road.

The minimum-deposit plan may appear attractive when only the tax deductibility of the loan interest is considered, but the plan may not appear so attractive when the potential income-tax consequences of terminating the plan many years in the future are considered.*

Financed insurance often is used to obscure a high-priced life insurance policy. Beware of the sales pitch that focuses primarily on the financing scheme. The subject of financing should not be discussed until the amount of insurance, the type of insurance, and the company have been selected.

Classic examples of the use of financed insurance to obscure the nature of the contract are found in the practices of some companies on college campuses. Frequently undergraduate students are sold a policy on the basis of "$10 down and no further payments until after you graduate." It is the rare student who understands the implications of the contract into which he or she has entered. Inappropriate, high-priced policies are often sold to students. And some students do not realize until it is too late that they signed promissory notes and are legally obligated to pay them.

Nor is campus solicitation limited to undergraduates. Graduate students are intensively solicited. And elaborate financing schemes have been developed for young professionals—such as budding physicians serving as interns or residents. Frequently these individuals are married and need large amounts of life insurance. The financing arrangements go well beyond minimum deposit, because a young doctor may borrow the full premium each year for several years— "nothing to pay until you get into practice."

Invariably the sale is straight life, so the doctor may build up a large amount of indebtedness that must be repaid during the trials and tribulations of starting a practice. A young doctor with large life insurance needs and limited funds is a candidate for one-year renewable term insurance. Even the relatively small premiums for this insurance may have to be financed; but by buying term insurance the doctor will build up a much smaller amount of indebtedness than would be the case if straight life were purchased.

---

*For a discussion of the potential income-tax consequences of terminating a minimum-deposit plan, see "Watch Out for Minnie Dee," *The Insurance Forum,* Vol. 2, No. 1 (January, 1975), p. 2.

Chapter 15

After the Life Insurance Purchase

Buyers of life insurance often tend to forget about a life insurance policy once it has been purchased, except for the sometimes painful need to pay a premium. Unfortunately, forgetting about a policy can be expensive as well as destructive of the purposes for which the coverage was bought. This chapter discusses several areas that should be kept in mind by the policyowner following the purchase of life insurance.

Periodic Review

Circumstances sometimes change rapidly, so it is important to review your life insurance program periodically. Ideally, you should review the program once a year. Failing that, try to do a thorough review at least once every two years. When you perform the review, you may be surprised at the number of changes you will want to make.

A good agent—if you are fortunate enough to have selected one—will encourage you to review your life insurance program periodically. But if your agent fails to take the initiative, do so yourself. Even if no additional sale materializes from the review, your agent should assist you with it. Your agent owes this service to you because of the commission he or she earned when you bought life insurance.

The beneficiary designation is one area that often requires periodic review, because of changes in family relationships. Consider, for example, the case of Harold and Ruth. Harold designated Ruth as beneficiary, if living, otherwise their two sons equally, or the survivor. This designation means that, if Ruth and one of their sons were to predecease Harold, the other son would receive all the funds at Harold's death. Years later, both sons were married and had families of their own. If Harold failed to change the beneficiary designation, if Ruth and one of their sons predeceased Harold, and if Harold then died, all the funds would go to the surviving son. The effect would be to disinherit their widowed daughter-in-law and their fatherless grandchildren. Presumably this would not be Harold's and Ruth's intent, but it would happen because they had failed to review the beneficiary designation.

The settlement agreement is another area that often requires periodic review. This subject was discussed in Chapter 9, and the importance of keeping such agreements up to date was illustrated by a discussion of an agreement that was found to be seriously outdated when the insured died.

Storage of Policies

A common practice is to keep one's life insurance policies in a safe-deposit box at a bank. You should not do so, however, because this procedure has some important disadvantages.

First, there may be delay in getting the policies in the event of the insured's death. Frequently a representative of the state's taxing authorities must inventory the contents of a deceased's safe-deposit box before making the contents available to the deceased's family.

Second, policies kept in a safe-deposit box probably will be looked at only rarely. The policyowner may procrastinate in reviewing the policies because they are not readily available.

For these reasons, it is preferable to keep your policies at home in a desk drawer or filing cabinet. If the policies are destroyed, stolen, or lost, you can obtain duplicate copies from the insurance companies. To expedite matters, make a list showing the names of the companies and the policy numbers. Keep the list—rather than the policies themselves—in a safe-deposit box. The policyowner who follows this procedure will have his or her policies more accessible and also will require a smaller, less expensive safe-deposit box.

Replacement of Life Insurance

The word "replacement" refers to the act of discontinuing a life insurance policy and taking out a new one in its place. A policyowner has the right of replacement if that is his or her desire. Despite what some would have you believe, nothing is inherently wrong or immoral about replacement, but as will be explained shortly, it is sometimes contrary to the policyowner's best interests.

For the life insurance business as a whole, replacements are counterproductive. They tend to increase certain expenses—commissions and other expenses associated with the issuance of new policies—without increasing the amount of life insurance in force. As a result, many companies are sensitive about replacements and try to discourage them.

A life insurance agent is said to be "twisting" if he or she uses misrepresentation or an incomplete comparison to induce a replacement to the detriment of the policyowner. State laws invariably prohibit twisting, and some states have regulations that require the disclosure of specified information to the policyowner in a replacement situation. Thus, when a replacement is proposed, the agent making the proposal may be required to furnish the policyowner with specified information about the existing policy and about the suggested replacement policy.

Presumably the purposes of the disclosure requirements are to spell out the kind of information the agent must furnish to avoid being accused of making an incomplete comparison, and to provide the policyowner with the information necessary for an intelligent decision. Unfortunately, however, the requirements result in nondisclosure, because the required information is neither condensed nor interpreted so that the policyowner can digest it. Furthermore, the completion of the necessary forms is such a difficult task that some agents are discouraged from proposing a replacement even when it is justified.

The inadequacy of the disclosure requirements in replacement situations is no accident. The requirements have been developed by representatives of the life insurance industry in closed meetings and adopted by the regulators with little or no change.

In recent years the shortcomings of the disclosure requirements have been so clearly recognized that a number of states have eliminated the requirements. In these states, all that is generally required is that the company whose policy may be replaced be informed. Then the company can attempt to prevent the replacement if it so desires. Little or no consideration has been given to improving the disclosure requirements to make them useful to consumers—because, as mentioned elsewhere in this book, the life insurance industry is opposed to the concept of rigorous disclosure to life insurance consumers.

One argument often made against replacement is that the policyowner incurs a second set of acquisition costs (the "front-end load") even though he or she has only one policy. This argument is valid as far as it goes, but those using the argument often fail to mention that price differences among policies are large. It is possible for a policyowner with a high-priced policy to be better off by incurring a second set of acquisition expenses in order to obtain a low-priced policy.

Another argument often made against replacement is that the incontestability and suicide periods begin again. This argument also is valid, but is of limited practical significance. Furthermore, it is interesting to note that the industry-developed replacement regulations generally do not frown upon replacement of term policies—only upon replacement of cash-value policies. Yet the incontestability and suicide clauses are as important in term policies as in cash-value policies. (See the discussions of these clauses in Chapters 9 and 10.)

A third argument often made against replacement is that the existing policy may contain clauses more favorable to the policyowner than those in the proposed replacement policy. This argument sounds reasonable, but today, with the exception of the loan clause, the proposed replacement policy is likely to have the more favorable clauses. Also, it is often difficult to determine the relative value of the various clauses.

The only valid generalization that can be made about replacement is that it is impossible to generalize. Sometimes replacement is justified, sometimes replacement is detrimental to the policyowner, and sometimes it makes little difference one way or the other. In short, any given replacement situation must be evaluated on the basis of its own set of facts.

In the face of this uncertainty, you should not replace a policy unless you are convinced that the replacement is to your advantage. Since the agent who recommends replacement has a vested financial interest in it—a new first-year commission—you should seek the advice of the company that wrote the original policy. Unfortunately, when and if you receive this advice, you may become confused by the conflicting assertions to which you are subjected. For that reason, Chapter 16 describes a procedure with which you can find out for yourself whether you should give serious consideration to replacement of an existing policy.

If you decide to replace your policy, follow the advice in this book so you will acquire a new policy from a financially strong company that provides low-priced protection containing favorable policy provisions. And be sure the new policy is in effect before you discontinue the old one. When in doubt, keep the old policy.

Finally, in some situations an existing policy is no longer appropriate. For example, you may have purchased a retirement income policy when you were single and now consider straight life more suitable because you are married and raising a family. Under such circumstances, instead of replacing the retirement income policy, consider changing it to a straight life policy as of its original issue date. (For a discussion of the change-of-plan provision, see Chapter 9.)

Filing the Death Claim

When the insured dies, the beneficiary does not have to act quickly in filing a death claim. Normally it is preferable to wait until the family has recovered from the initial shock of the loss of a loved one.

In the usual situation, it is not necessary for the beneficiary to pay anyone to collect the funds payable under a life insurance policy. Unless there is some dispute concerning the policy, it would be wasteful for the beneficiary to retain an attorney and pay a legal fee to obtain the life insurance proceeds. All the beneficiary has to do is notify the insurance company—or an agent—of the insured's death. The company will then provide the necessary forms and instructions.

If the beneficiary decides upon a single-sum settlement of the policy, the company will send a check shortly after receiving the policy, the death certificate, and the death claim. If the beneficiary decides upon a settlement option, the company will send a "supplementary contract" that spells out the terms of the agreement between the beneficiary and the insurance company.

If the insured had selected and worked with a good life insurance agent, the beneficiary should turn to the agent. The details can be handled by the agent, who can also provide guidance to the beneficiary without a fee.

Complaint Procedures

When a dispute arises between an insurance company and a policyowner (or beneficiary), and when the dispute is not resolved by writing to a top company official, it is appropriate to contact the insurance department in the policyowner's state of residence. (The addresses of the various state insurance departments are listed in Appendix C.)

Don't hesitate to contact your state insurance department; it is equipped to handle complaints. It can act as an intermediary between the policyowner (or beneficiary) and the insurance company; often it can resolve disputes quickly and to the satisfaction of both parties. When you contact the insurance department, do so in writing. Explain the circumstances clearly but with reasonable brevity. Attach to your letter copies (keep the originals) of all relevant documents so that department officials will understand the dispute.

If you fail to get satisfaction through your state insurance department, it is appropriate to consult an attorney. Don't hesitate to take this step if you are genuinely dissatisfied. In some instances, an insurance company will quickly alter its stance when it receives a letter from an attorney representing the policyowner or beneficiary.

Another step that often yields prompt results is to write a letter to the "hot line" or "action line" of your local newspaper or television station. Insurance companies try to avoid adverse publicity, so you may obtain prompt satisfaction when you follow this procedure.

Finally, another possible step is to write to your state and/or federal legislators. Insurance companies lobby extensively in state capitols and in Washington, and they try to look good in the eyes of legislators. For that reason, you may be able to resolve your dispute quickly through the offices of your legislators.

Don't threaten your insurance company. If you are dissatisfied, don't threaten to write to your state insurance department—write to the department. Don't threaten to retain an attorney—retain one. Don't threaten to contact the media—do so. Don't threaten to write to your legislators—write to them. Action speaks louder than words.

Chapter 16

How to Evaluate an Existing Life Insurance Policy

You may own one or more life insurance policies on which you have paid premiums for several years. If you are wondering whether you are receiving fair value for your money, this chapter will help you answer the question.

Many of those in the life insurance business are legitimate and ethical sales people; however, the business is plagued by a significant number of replacement artists and conservation artists. A replacement artist is a person who uses dubious methods to convince you—the owner of an existing policy—to replace your policy with a new one. Some replacement artists attempt to discredit the agent and the company from whom you bought your policy. Some of what replacement artists say may be accurate, but some of it may be deceptive or even false. The problem is that most policyowners cannot determine what is and is not accurate.

A conservation artist, on the other hand, is a person who uses dubious methods to convince you that your policy should not be replaced. Some conservation artists attempt to discredit anyone who proposes a replacement, irrespective of whether replacement is warranted. Some of what conservation artists say may be accurate, but some of it may be deceptive or even false. The problem is that most policyowners cannot determine what is and is not accurate.

In short, a war is going on between replacement artists and conservation artists. As the owner of a life insurance policy, you are caught in the middle. You probably do not know enough about life insurance to be able to distinguish accurate from inaccurate information, and you probably do not know whom to believe.

The purpose of this chapter is to arm you with the ability to find out for yourself whether the life insurance protection you own is reasonably priced, and, if your life insurance contains a savings component, whether you are receiving a reasonable rate of return. Three steps must be followed. First, you must gather raw data about each policy you want to evaluate. Second, you must perform calculations using the data gathered in the first step. Third, you must evaluate the results of your calculations.

Gathering Information

The most difficult step is not doing the arithmetic, but assembling the necessary information. Some of what you need is in the policy itself, but the information often is difficult to extract. And some of what you need may not be in the policy. You should obtain the information by writing a precisely worded letter to the president of the life insurance company that issued the policy. A sample letter is shown in Figure 7.

You can find the address of the company on the policy, on a recent premium notice, by calling your local library, or by contacting your state insurance department. (The addresses of the state insurance

Figure 7
Sample Letter Requesting Information about an Existing Policy

1234 North Main Street
Bloomington, IN 47401
June 1, 1985

Mr. Steven S. Smith, President
ABC Life Insurance Company
5678 South Elm Street
Philadelphia, PA 19101

Dear Mr. Smith:

I am evaluating policy number 123456, of which I am the owner. In that connection, I need the following information:

1. The amount you would have paid in a single sum to the beneficiary if the insured had died at the end of the most recently completed policy year. Please exclude the death benefits of any riders. Please also exclude the effect of any dividends and any loan against the policy.

2. The amount you would have paid in a single sum to me if I had surrendered the policy at the end of the most recently completed policy year. Please exclude the effect of any dividends and any loan against the policy.

3. The amount you would have paid in a single sum to me if I had surrendered the policy at the end of the year preceding the most recently completed policy year. Please exclude the effect of any dividends and any loan against the policy.

4. The annual premium for the most recently completed policy year. Please exclude the premiums for any riders. Please also exclude the interest on any loan against the policy, and assume the year's premium was paid in full at the beginning of the year.

5. The annual dividend for the most recently completed policy year. Please exclude the dividends attributable to any riders. Please also exclude the dividends attributable to any dividend additions and the interest on any dividend accumulation.

6. The date on which the most recently completed policy year began

7. The age of the insured, according to your records, when the most recently completed policy year began.

Also, please furnish the above data for the two policy years preceding the most recently completed policy year, and for the two policy years following the most recently completed policy year. In the case of amounts payable in future years, please identify any nonguaranteed amounts and base the figures on your current scale.

It would be helpful if you would provide the requested information on the enclosed form. If you provide a computer printout, please indicate which figures belong in the various spaces of the enclosed form. Thank you for providing the information that I have requested.

Sincerely yours,

John J. Jones

Enclosure

departments are listed in Appendix C.) You can find the policy number on the policy or on a recent premium notice.

Some companies respond to the letter in such a way as to make it difficult for consumers to sort out the information provided. For that reason, you should send the form in Figure 8 with the letter. If the company provides the information by completing the form, it will be a simple matter for you to make the necessary calculations.*

Keep a copy of your letter. If you receive no response, or if you receive an inadequate response, file a complaint with your state insurance department. The procedure for filing a complaint is described in Chapter 15.

If you own more than one policy in a particular company, use a separate letter and form for each policy you want to evaluate. Your letter should request the following items of information:

(1) The amount the insurance company would have paid to the beneficiary if the insured had died at the end of the most recently completed policy year. This is the death benefit (DB) of the policy.

(2) The amount the insurance company would have paid to you if you had surrendered the policy at the end of the most recently completed policy year. This is the cash value (CV) of the policy. (Some policies do not have cash values, so the amount here could be zero.)

(3) The amount the insurance company would have paid to you if you had surrendered the policy at the end of the year preceding the most recently completed policy year. This (CVP) corresponds to item 2, but for one year earlier.

(4) The annual premium (P) for the most recently completed policy year. (Policies that are "paid up" require no further premiums, so the amount here could be zero.)

(5) The annual dividend (D) for the most recently completed policy year. (Some policies do not pay dividends, so the amount here could be zero.)

(6) The date on which the most recently completed policy year began.

---

*Permission is hereby granted to reproduce the form in Figure 8. Also, an 8½ × 11 reprint of the form is available. Send a stamped, addressed envelope to the author at P. O. Box 245, Ellettsville, IN 47429, and request the data form for an existing policy.

Figure 8
Form for Recording Information about an Existing Policy

Company _____

Policy No. _____

Owner _____

	Year A	Year B	Year C	Year D	Year E
(1) Death benefit (DB)					
(2) Cash value end of year (CV)					
(3) Cash value end of preceding year (CVP)					
(4) Annual premium (P)					
(5) Annual dividend (D)					
(6) Date on which policy year began					
(7) Age of insured on above date					
(8) Yearly price (YPT)					
(9) Benchmark price					

Year A: Second year before most recently completed policy year.

Year B: Year before most recently completed policy year.

Year C: Most recently completed policy year.

Year D: Year after most recently completed policy year.

Year E: Second year after most recently completed policy year.

(7) The age of the insured, in accordance with the company's method of determining age, on the date referred to in item 6.

Note that your letter also should request this information for the two years preceding the most recently completed policy year, and for the two years following the most recently completed policy year. If your policy is less than three years old, modify the letter and request the information for any years preceding the most recently completed policy year, and for more than two years following the most recently completed policy year.

The Price Calculations

Once you have acquired the information referred to in the preceding section, you are ready to pei form the price calculations, except for the choice of an assumed interest rate (i). You should assume an interest rate of 6 percent (.06) in your calculations. (For a discussion of the choice of the assumed interest rate, see Appendix D.)

Now you are ready to perform the calculations necessary to arrive at yearly prices per $1,000 of protection for the most recently completed policy year, and for two years on each side of that year. The formula is the same as that shown on page 79 in Chapter 8, and is explained in Appendix D.

To illustrate, suppose the response to your letter provides the following information for the most recently completed policy year:

(1) Death benefit (DB): $25,000
(2) Cash value at end of most recently completed policy year (CV): $10,450
(3) Cash value at end of year preceding most recently completed policy year (CVP): $10,000
(4) Annual premium (P): $550
(5) Annual dividend (D): $400
(6) Date on which most recently completed policy year began: March 10, 1984
(7) Your insurance age on March 10, 1984: 56

Your next step is to plug these figures into the formula. The calculations are as follows:

$$YPT = \frac{(550 + 10,000)(1 + .06) - (10,450 + 400)}{(25,000 - 10,450)(.001)}$$

$$= \frac{(10,550)(1.06) - 10,850}{(14,550)(.001)}$$

$$= \frac{11,183 - 10,850}{14.550} = \frac{333}{14.550} = 22.89$$

Stated verbally, the yearly price per $1,000 of protection in the most recently completed policy year (which began on March 10, 1984) is $22.89, assuming 6 percent interest. Similar calculations should be performed for the two years on each side of that year.

Evaluating the Prices

The benchmarks against which to compare yearly prices per $1,000 of protection are shown in Table 9 on page 84. The suggested interpretations are as follows:

- If the yearly price per $1,000 of protection is less than the benchmark, the price of your protection is low, and you should not consider replacing your policy.
- If the yearly price per $1,000 of protection is more than the benchmark but less than double the benchmark, the price of your protection is moderate, and again you should not consider replacing your policy.
- If the yearly price per $1,000 of protection is more than double the benchmark, the price of your protection is high, and you should consider replacing your policy.

To illustrate, the benchmark for age 56 is $15, and the yearly price per $1,000 of protection that came out of your calculations is $22.89. Since the latter is more than the benchmark but less than double the benchmark, the price of your protection is moderate, and you should not consider replacing the policy.

The Rate-of-Return Calculations

If your policy contains a savings component, yearly rates of return on that savings component may be calculated using the information referred to earlier in this chapter. To perform the calculations, you must assume a yearly price per $1,000 of protection (YPT). Use the price figure corresponding to your age in Table 9 on page 84. For age 56, for example, the figure is $15.

Now you are ready to perform some calculations to arrive at a yearly rate of return on the savings component for the most recently completed policy year. The formula is the same as that shown on page 90 in Chapter 8, and is explained in Appendix E.

To illustrate, suppose the response to your letter provided the same information shown earlier for the most recently completed policy year. Your next step is to plug these figures into the formula. The calculations are as follows:

$$i = \frac{(10,450 + 400) + (15)(25,000 - 10,450)(.001)}{(550 + 10,000)} - 1$$

$$= \frac{(10,850) + (15)(14,550)(.001)}{(10,550)} - 1$$

$$= \frac{10,850 + 218}{10,550} - 1$$

$$= \frac{11,068}{10,550} - 1 = 1.049 - 1 = .049 = 4.9\%$$

Note that the formula produces a rate of return expressed as a decimal (.049), which may be converted to a percentage by moving the decimal point two places to the right. Stated verbally, the yearly rate of return on the savings component in the most recently completed policy year (which began on March 10, 1984) is 4.9 percent, assuming $15 is the yearly price per $1,000 of protection. Similar calculations should be performed for the two years on each side of the most recently completed policy year.

You should use the procedure for calculating yearly prices per $1,000 of protection when considering the question of whether to replace an existing policy. Use the procedure for calculating yearly rates of return solely to determine whether you are receiving a reasonable rate of return on the savings component of your cash-value life insurance. To evaluate the results of your rate-of-return calculations, follow the procedure described in Chapter 8.

Several Warnings

Life insurance policies are complex financial instruments. In this chapter, an attempt has been made to simplify the subject so that you can find out for yourself whether your life insurance protection is reasonably priced, and, if your life insurance contains a savings component, whether you are receiving a reasonable rate of return. The simplification process, however, makes it necessary to voice several warnings.

Policy Loans

The system of policy evaluation described in this chapter does not account for any policy loan that may be outstanding. The system is based on the notion that a policy loan is a separate transaction; if a policy loan exists on your policy, you may want to evaluate it as a separate transaction.

It would be possible to develop a system that specifically builds policy loans into the analysis; however, such a system would be more complicated than the system described in this chapter. If you use an assumed interest rate of 6 percent in the price calculations, as suggested, and if the policy loan interest rate is 6 percent, the existence of a policy loan will not alter the results. In other words, a policy loan affects the results of the system described in this chapter only to the extent that the policy loan interest rate differs from the interest rate assumed in the price calculations.

Dividends

The system of policy evaluation described in this chapter does not account for the effect of dividends left with the insurance company. If you have left dividends with the company, you may want to evaluate your dividend account as a separate transaction. For example, if you have left dividends with the company to accumulate at interest, you may want to compare the interest rate paid by the company with the interest rates available to you in savings banks, savings and loan associations, and credit unions. If you have left dividends with the company to purchase paid-up additions, you may want to evaluate the price of the protection in those additions. To do so, you should treat the additions as small, separate purchases of single-premium life insurance, and follow the procedure described in Chapter 8.

It would be possible to develop a system that builds in the effect of dividends left with the company; however, such a system would be more complicated than the system described in this chapter. If you use 6 percent interest in your price calculations, as suggested, and if you earn 6 percent interest on your dividend accumulations, they will have no effect on the results of the system described in this chapter. In other words, they affect the results only to the extent that the interest rate paid differs from the interest rate assumed in the calculations. As for dividend additions, they affect the results only to the extent that the price of the protection in the additions differs from the price of the protection in the basic policy.

Certain Policy Types

The system of evaluation described in this chapter cannot be applied to certain types of policies. For example, if your policy carries an extra premium because of a health impairment or other problem, the analysis of that policy is beyond the scope of the system. Similarly, if your policy covers more than one life, the analysis of that policy also is beyond the scope of the system. (See Chapter 4 for a discussion of multi-life policies.)

If yours is a small policy—with less than, say, a $3,000 death benefit—the yearly prices per $1,000 of protection may be high because of the expenses associated with the maintenance of a small policy. It may not be worth the bother to replace a small policy; indeed, a small policy may not be worth keeping unless you have some emotional attachment to it.

Unusual Years

It is possible that the primary year for which you perform the calculations—the most recently completed policy year—is not representative of other years. For example, the price of the protection in the first one or two years is often high, reflecting sales commissions and the other expenses associated with the issuance of a life insurance policy. As another example, the price in a single isolated year may be low or high because of certain structural characteristics of the policy.

For these reasons, you should perform the calculations for at least a few other years. The suggested letter and form are designed to help you obtain the necessary information not only for the most recently completed policy year, but also for two years on each side of that year.

Negative Results

In the calculation of the yearly price per $1,000 of protection, you may obtain a negative result. This may arise because of an unusual year, as mentioned above, or because the price of the protection in your policy is very low. A negative figure does not mean the company is confused—remember that you are using an interest rate of 6 percent in your calculations and that the company may be earning a higher interest rate on its investments.

In the calculation of the yearly rate of return, you also may obtain a negative result. This may arise because of an unusual year, as mentioned above, or because the rate of return on the savings component of your policy is very low.

Little or No Protection

If the cash value of your policy is equal to the death benefit, you have no life insurance protection, and the yearly price per $1,000 of protection is without meaning. Under these circumstances, you should view your policy as a savings account. Calculate the yearly rate of return (expressed as a decimal) with the following formula:

$$i = \frac{CV + D}{P + CVP} - 1$$

where i is the yearly rate of return expressed as a decimal, and the other items are the same as in the formulas discussed in Chapter 8.

You can then judge your policy by comparing the yearly rate of return with what you can earn in a savings bank, savings and loan association, or credit union. When you make such a comparison, however, you should consider the income tax situation, which was discussed in Chapters 5 and 8.

If the cash value of your policy is only slightly smaller than the death benefit (less than, say, 5 percent below the death benefit), you have little life insurance protection, and the yearly price per $1,000 of protection has little meaning. Under these circumstances, you should view your policy essentially as a savings account. Use the above formula to approximate the yearly rate of return.

A General Warning

In the section of this chapter concerning evaluation of the yearly prices, it was suggested that, if the price of the protection in your policy is high, you should consider replacing your policy. It was not suggested that you should necessarily replace your policy.

There are several reasons for you to proceed with caution: a replacement involves the purchase of a new policy, and the purchase of a new policy requires care if you want to acquire suitable, low-priced protection; surrendering an existing policy may involve the sacrifice of valuable policy provisions; surrendering an existing policy may involve income tax considerations; purchasing a new policy may involve significant expenses in the first one or two years; and because of a health impairment or other problem, you may find it difficult to qualify for a new policy.

Chapter 17

Conclusion

Ignorance, complexity, and apathy are the three words that best characterize the market for individual life insurance. One purpose of this chapter is to describe these characteristics and show how their combined effect produces fertile ground for the exploitation of life insurance consumers. Another purpose of this chapter is to explain what is and is not being done to improve the market for the benefit of life insurance consumers.

Ignorance

Many prospective buyers do not understand the different kinds of life insurance policies. They do not know some life insurance companies are operating with inadequate financial resources. They do not know there are large price differences among life insurance companies for essentially the same coverage. They have not examined the financial implications of the death of a breadwinner, and they do not appreciate fully the important role of life insurance at such a time. It is hoped that this book will dispel some of the ignorance among life insurance consumers.

Nor is ignorance confined to life insurance consumers. Many life insurance agents are ill-equipped to provide reliable financial advice for their customers. Indeed, many life insurance agents are almost as ignorant about many aspects of life insurance as are their prospects. State licensing examinations require a minimum of knowledge about life insurance. Some agent organizations have recommended mandatory continuing education, and these requirements are in effect in a few states; however, mandatory continuing education is opposed by many life insurance companies and by many life insurance agents.

Company training programs for agents and most industry-wide training programs place the emphasis on sales skill rather than technical knowledge. An exception is the Chartered Life Underwriter (CLU) program, which requires the candidate to absorb a substantial body of technical material. However, the holders of the CLU designation still comprise a minority of the life insurance agents.

Nor is ignorance confined to life insurance buyers and life insurance agents. Many life insurance company home office executives have only a superficial knowledge of life insurance. Life insurance company investment officers and many life insurance company attorneys are engaged in specialized work that has only an indirect effect on the life insurance market. And those responsible for sales development generally have come up through the sales ranks. Many of these sales executives were successful in the field, but sales success is not synonymous with technical knowledge. Indeed, it is sometimes said that technical knowledge tends to hamper sales efforts.

Those who know the most about life insurance, and who must therefore assume the primary responsibility for the ignorance in the life insurance market, are the actuaries. These are the technicians of life insurance. They are responsible for the calculation of premiums, cash values, and dividends. They are responsible for the calculation of life insurance reserves, which are important in determining the financial position of a life insurance company. They do the technical work in the development of new policies. Their knowledge and expertise are used in virtually every aspect of life insurance company operations. Although they are company employees, they subscribe to a code of professional conduct. Those who complete a comprehensive series of examinations become Fellows of the Society of Actuaries and are allowed to display the FSA designation after their names.

In defense of the actuaries, many of them are not in a strong enough position to affect company policy. Suppose an actuary makes a recommendation that benefits consumers. If implementation of the recommendation may have an adverse effect upon the company's profits or sales volume—even if the adverse effect is likely to be temporary—it may be sidetracked by other executives. If an actuary's recommendations are repeatedly sidetracked, he or she may become less enthusiastic about making them. The actuary may decide it is safer to follow the path of least resistance. The result is likely to be a continuation of the status quo.

The position of the actuary is illustrated by some comments contained in an eight-page letter written in 1979 by James F. Reiskytl, FSA, an actuary at The Northwestern Mutual Life Insurance Company. The letter was written to the chairman of a committee formed to give advice to the National Association of Insurance Commissioners on the subject of manipulation. (Manipulation may be defined, for the purposes of this discussion, as the act of using questionable actuarial practices to make life insurance policies look better than they deserve to look.) Two paragraphs of Mr. Reiskytl's letter read:

> The public record shows that there are mutual companies that have not changed their dividend scales for blocks of old business for long periods of time, some as long as 20 years. At the same time, these companies have introduced improved illustrated dividends for new issues every few years. Thus, old policyholders have received no share of improving mortality and higher investment earnings, even though such improvements are passed along to successive new groups. At best it may be some sort of half-baked, undefined investment year method. At least it appears to clearly qualify as malignant manipulation.
>
> We know that often the actuaries of these companies have been concerned, but they have received no support from their companies, nor from the regulators, nor even from the actuarial profession. Nobody cares. We think it is time somebody cared!*

---

*"The Actuaries of 'The Quiet Company' Assume a Leadership Role," *The Insurance Forum*, Vol. 6, No. 6 (June, 1979), pp. 1–2.

The position of the actuary is also illustrated by the response of the actuarial profession to the subject of deceptive practices used in the sale of life insurance. Several years ago, a committee that deals with the professional responsibility of actuaries was asked to address the question of whether the actuary should take positive action to prevent deceptive sales practices, or whether the actuary should merely refrain from endorsing such practices. The committee declined to answer the question. A member of the committee explained that the committee would have been embarrassed to recommend that the actuary should merely refrain from endorsing deceptive sales practices. But a recommendation that the actuary should take positive action would mean that many actuaries would have to resign their positions. So the committee decided that the appropriate decision was to decline to answer the question.

Complexity

The complexity of life insurance reinforces the ignorance referred to in the preceding section of this chapter. Two kinds of life insurance complexity, however, relate directly to consumers.

The first of these is the complexity that is inherent in life insurance because of its nature and purpose. Death rates increase with advancing age; therefore, in the absence of special arrangements, premiums increase with advancing age. When special arrangements are made to avoid increasing premiums, the resulting level premiums involve overcharges that give rise to a savings component. Cash-value life insurance policies, therefore, are complex packages consisting of a life insurance protection component and a savings component.

Furthermore, because the premium for a life insurance policy is small in relation to the policy's death benefit, safeguards must be incorporated into life insurance to protect the companies and their policyowners from attempts to defraud. The effect of these safeguards is an increase in complexity. It is hoped that this book will help consumers deal with the complexity inherent in life insurance.

The second kind of life insurance complexity stems from the proliferation of policy types. It is not surprising that there are many life insurance policy types, because companies in every business (other than the monopolies) engage in product differentiation not only to offer a better product but also to avoid price competition.

But the proliferation in life insurance has reached large proportions. For example, many specialty policies are designed to fit an elaborate sales presentation, rather than to perform services for the buyer. Indeed, some of these policies are so complex that they appear to have been designed to make it impossible for buyers to understand them. There are also many different policies of the conventional type—so many, indeed, that it is difficult to distinguish between conventional policies and specialty policies.

Here again, it is hoped that this book will help consumers. One of the major premises of the book is that the life insurance needs of nearly all buyers can be met satisfactorily by just two policy forms—one-year renewable term and straight life—or some of each.

Apathy

Apathy is widespread in the life insurance market. The typical person does not like to talk about life insurance, because it forces the person to think about his or her death. People would rather spend their leisure time discussing automobiles, sports, politics, social problems, or the state of the economy.

Apathy is important in at least two respects. First, it is at least partially responsible for what happens in the life insurance market. The effect of the apathy is to make life insurance difficult to sell. This difficulty, in turn, makes it necessary for life insurance companies to provide intensive sales training for their agents. Since the companies want their agents in production quickly, there is not enough time for the agents to receive a thorough grounding in the technical aspects of life insurance. Moreover, as noted, a feeling prevails that technical knowledge does not assist, and may actually hinder, sales efforts.

Once the agent starts to sell, he or she is likely to encounter difficulty in maintaining satisfactory production. The selling problems usually stem from apathy on the part of prospective buyers. So the agent must be provided with constant encouragement and more sales training. The constant emphasis on sales techniques, moreover, probably tends to harden the resistance of buyers. Many buyers are turned off by "the hard sell." So the agents are given still more sales training to overcome the sales resistance of their prospects. In short, apathy on the part of buyers is at least partially responsible for the emphasis on sales tactics as well as the kind of sales tactics employed by life insurance companies and their agents.

The second important effect of apathy on the life insurance market is that it tends to perpetuate ignorance. When people are not interested in discussing life insurance, they do not find out how it operates or how it can be useful to them. They do not learn of major differences among policies and among companies. They get the idea that all life insurance is the same.

Thus, there is a circular characteristic to the ignorance, complexity, and apathy that permeate the life insurance market. Apathy fosters ignorance and complexity, because consumers generally are not interested enough in life insurance to try to dispel their ignorance and cut through the complexity. At the same time, ignorance and complexity foster apathy, because consumers generally do not realize the extent to which they are penalized by ignorance and complexity and therefore are not interested in life insurance.

The Results

In this kind of atmosphere, opportunities for the exploitation of consumers abound. Some companies train their agents to use a single sales presentation designed to sell one particular policy, without consideration of the suitability of the policy for a particular buyer. Many such policies are high-priced as well as unsuitable, and their primary redeeming virtues are a large agent's commission and an even larger profit for the insurance company.

Some companies are allowed to continue operations even though they are in precarious financial condition. As long as buyers think all insurance companies are financially strong, and as long as the insurance departments in many states are unable or unwilling to do an adequate job in this area, these companies will continue to take premium dollars from unsuspecting consumers.

Even if they acquire suitable life insurance from financially strong companies, many policyowners are overcharged, in the sense that they could have bought comparable coverage from equally strong companies at much lower prices. How can large price differences exist? The market for individual life insurance is characterized by an absence of reliable price information. As long as buyers think all life insurance companies charge about the same price, companies that charge high prices can sell as successfully as companies that charge low prices.

Fortunately, some financially strong companies sell life insurance at low prices, and some agents do a good job of selecting suitable policies to meet the needs of their customers. It is hoped that this book will help you find such companies, agents, and policies.

The life insurance market is characterized not only by an absence of reliable price information, but also by the presence of deceptive price information. The word "deceptive," as used here, refers to information that tends to give the buyer an erroneous impression of important relationships. The emphasis is on the buyer, and it is not intended to suggest that the deception is necessarily deliberate on the part of the company or agent. Many companies and agents engage in deceptive sales practices without realizing it.

Suppose a 25-year-old man has decided to buy $100,000 of life insurance to cover the next forty years. He is told he can pay $1,000 per year for forty years, a total of $40,000; or he can pay $2,000 per year for the first ten years and nothing thereafter, a total of $20,000. The agent tells him he should take the second payment arrangement because it is half as costly as the first arrangement. However, when the timing of the payments is considered, the two payment arrangements have about the same value.

The kind of deception referred to in the preceding paragraph—where amounts payable at different times are added without consideration of their timing, and where the results are then compared—is generally understood to be improper. Unfortunately, this type of deception is still widespread. Some states prohibit these presentations, but generally the prohibitions are not enforced. And some states have not adopted these prohibitions.

Even more serious is price information given to consumers regarding one policy year at a time. An agent might say that in the tenth year of a given policy the premium (minus the dividend, if any) is smaller than the amount by which the cash value increases that year. The agent then says the policyowner's cost that year is negative. The problem stems from an improper handling of the interest factor.

The kind of deception referred to in the preceding paragraph—where the interest factor is improperly allocated in an analysis of a single policy year—is not prohibited in any state, and remains widespread today. One state—New York—adopted a rule several years ago prohibiting these presentations, but did not enforce it. The rule was quietly repealed a few years ago.*

Some deceptive practices provide the consumer with exaggerated

---

*"The Saga of New York's Regulation 74," *The Insurance Forum*, Vol. 7, No. 6 (June, 1980), pp. 3–4.

figures purporting to represent the rate of return on the savings component of cash-value life insurance. For example, in the case of universal life, it is standard practice to emphasize the rate of interest being credited to the cash values without a corresponding emphasis on the expense charges imposed by the company. The result is that the consumer sees figures such as 12 percent, which is a gross interest rate, but does not see the net interest rates after the expense charges are taken into account. Such net interest rates often are substantially below the gross interest rate.

The kind of deception referred to in the preceding paragraph—where the emphasis is placed on gross interest rates rather than net interest rates—is not prohibited in any state. Late in 1984, an advisory committee to the National Association of Insurance Commissioners began deliberations on how to deal with the problem.

These and other deceptive practices are widespread. They are so varied and so complex that it is impractical for the consumer to attempt to recognize them. You should follow carefully the procedures described in this book and disregard any figures that deviate from those procedures.

What Is Being Done?

The only effective way to make reliable price information widely available to life insurance consumers is through a rigorous system of information disclosure. The need for this kind of system was suggested in a 1966 study.* In the years since, there has been an endless succession of studies, debates, hearings, reports, proposals, bills, and regulations.

Perhaps the most important event in the life insurance disclosure movement was a 1968 speech by the late United States Senator Philip A. Hart (D-MI), who at the time was chairman of the Subcommittee on Antitrust and Monopoly of the Committee on the Judiciary. Senator Hart's interest in the subject was stimulated by the life insurance problems of veterans of the Vietnam War. Personnel in military service at that time were provided automatically with some life insurance protection. Upon discharge, a veteran who wanted to continue the insurance had to convert the coverage into a regular policy in any one

---

*Joseph M. Belth, *The Retail Price Structure in American Life Insurance* (Bloomington, IN: Indiana University School of Business, 1966).

of several hundred life insurance companies. However, the veteran was provided with no guidance whatever to assist in the selection of quality coverage at a low price. Senator Hart asked the Veterans' Administration to gather the information necessary to assist veterans in making a sound choice. On July 10, 1968, the VA declined Senator Hart's request.

On October 15, 1968, Senator Hart addressed a group of life insurance attorneys in Chicago. In the speech he mentioned the possibility of "truth in life insurance" legislation. Here are a few of his comments:

> Obviously, if it makes sense to tell consumers how much of what is in a package on a supermarket shelf, or how much interest they will pay for using someone else's money, it makes sense to tell them how much they are paying for death protection and how much they are saving when they plunk down a life insurance premium.
>
> Hopefully your industry will think so too—and start supplying the information.
>
> If not—watch for Truth in Life Insurance to follow Truth in Packaging and Truth in Lending through the legislative mill.
>
> Because that's the way people are thinking in consumerland.

Early in 1969, as a direct result of Senator Hart's admonition, three life insurance trade associations appointed a prestigious industry committee to look into the price disclosure problem. The report of the committee was dated May 4, 1970. The major recommendation of the committee was that the traditional net-cost method—which involves the simple addition of amounts payable at different times—should be replaced by the interest-adjusted method—which recognizes the timing of payments by taking interest into account. The report did not go very far, but for the staid life insurance business it was a bombshell. It was so controversial that the trade associations who had appointed the committee did not endorse the report, but merely allowed it to be published.

In June 1972, Herbert S. Denenberg, who at the time was the insurance commissioner in Pennsylvania, published the first in a series of insurance shoppers' guides. It was on life insurance, and ranked companies by the prices of their policies using the interest-adjusted method. Although the guide was open to criticism in certain technical respects, it was a pioneering effort and became a media sensation. Hundreds of thousands of copies were distributed to consumers.

On February 20, 1973, Senator Hart began his first set of hearings on life insurance price disclosure. Although the hearings were purely exploratory, they had the effect of putting pressure on the state regulators to do something about the disclosure problem.

Later in 1973, the National Association of Insurance Commissioners (NAIC) adopted an interim model regulation providing for disclosure to life insurance consumers. The model was seriously deficient, and was adopted in only a few states; however, it was a landmark in the history of life insurance disclosure. The NAIC also took steps to study the subject with the objective of developing a more satisfactory model regulation.

On May 4, 1976, the NAIC adopted a more elaborate model disclosure regulation. Although a substantial amount of research was conducted between 1973 and 1976, the new model was not significantly better than the interim model. Indeed, the 1976 model provides for pseudo (fake) disclosure. Among the shortcomings of the model are its failure to require disclosure of (1) price information that would disclose the magnitude of the front-end load, (2) price information beyond twenty policy years, (3) information about the rate of return on the savings component, and (4) information on an annual basis to the owners of existing policies.

The life insurance business supported the 1976 model and lobbied successfully for its adoption in many states. Today more than half the states have life insurance disclosure regulations identical or similar to the 1976 model.

On July 10, 1979, the Federal Trade Commission made public its staff report on life insurance price disclosure. The report recommended that a rigorous system of disclosure be adopted by the states, and that the system include a requirement for disclosing information about the rate of return on the savings component in cash-value life insurance. The report so infuriated the life insurance business that it harnessed its political clout and (with the help of several other industries displeased with the FTC) persuaded Congress to order the FTC not to investigate the insurance business unless specifically asked to do so by one of the commerce committees.

On November 5, 1980, a task force of the NAIC made public a report recommending a new system of disclosure for the life insurance business. The proposed model regulation was extraordinary. Although there were technical deficiencies in the proposal, the approach embodied in the proposed model would have resulted in

rigorous disclosure for life insurance consumers. The following comments were included in a draft report prepared by the task force:

> As the task force began its work, few if any members contemplated that
> it would arrive at the recommendations contained in this report. Its initial
> work seemed to be aimed at refining and polishing the 1976 model regula-
> tion. But as the hearings unfolded and the deliberations proceeded, there
> was a growing realization that the current system is seriously flawed. De-
> spite its reluctance to depart dramatically from the general approach of
> the 1976 model, the task force arrived at the conclusion that life insurance
> disclosure is too fundamental, too important to consumers, industry, and
> regulators to continue to rest on a significantly defective base. The task
> force did not undertake this assignment with preconceived notions. Its
> opinions have, however, undergone substantial metamorphosis. It has
> reached these conclusions after long and intense deliberation. The task
> force firmly believes that its conclusions are soundly conceived and that
> their implementation will benefit the industry as well as the insurance-
> buying public.

When the report was made public, the task force included some
changes in the language of the report. For example, the phrase
"seriously flawed" was changed to "seriously deficient." The changes,
however, did not alter the thrust of the report.

The life insurance business was furious. It attacked the proposed
regulation, and offered no suggestions for its improvement. The proposal was shelved, and has not reappeared.

H. P. Hudson, who was the Indiana insurance commissioner and a
former president of the NAIC, chaired the task force. Shortly after
the report was made public, Commissioner Hudson was fired by Governor Robert D. Orr of Indiana. Commissioner Hudson's work on life
insurance disclosure may not have been the sole reason for his firing,
but it probably was a contributing factor.

The life insurance business did not stop with the sacking of Commissioner Hudson. Two staff persons at the central office of the
NAIC had worked extensively in the disclosure area. One of them was
hired by a major life insurance trade association. The other was fired.
Again, their work on life insurance disclosure may not have been the
main reason for these moves, but it probably was a contributing
factor.

In the past few years, no significant developments in the life insurance disclosure area have occurred. The various regulators appar-

ently realize how sensitive the subject is, and are intimidated by the life insurance industry.

It now appears there will never be a rigorous system of disclosure mandated for the life insurance industry. The industry is opposed to rigorous disclosure, and has enough influence to destroy any politician or regulatory agency with the temerity to propose it.

The Bottom Line

Buyers of new life insurance and owners of existing policies need certain information to make intelligent decisions in their own interests. Because there probably will never be a rigorous system of disclosure mandated for the life insurance industry, there is only one way you can get the necessary information. You must take the initiative and obtain the information yourself.

This book is designed to help you obtain the information you need. Your objective should be to buy and own an appropriate amount and an appropriate type of life insurance that is issued by a financially strong company, that is low priced, and that contains favorable provisions. If you follow the suggestions and the procedures described in this book, you should achieve that objective. And if you achieve that objective, you will have done well in your life insurance planning.

Appendixes

Appendix A
Computation of Present Values

The purpose of this appendix is to explain how to calculate the present value of your income needs and the present value of your estimated Social Security survivors' benefits. The phrase "present value" means the amount of funds which, if available at the beginning of a time period and consistently invested at an assumed interest rate, would be precisely sufficient to produce the given yearly payments. For example, Table 12 shows that $10,295 would be the present value of $1,000 per year for fifteen years at 6 percent interest. In other words, $10,295 would be precisely sufficient to produce payments of $1,000 per year for fifteen years (with the payments at the beginning of each year), if the remaining funds were consistently invested at 6 percent interest, compounded annually.

Table 12 shows the present value of $1,000 per year (with the payments at the beginning of each year) for various numbers of years at various interest rates. The table can be used to calculate not only the present value of a series of equal payments but also the present value of a series of unequal payments. Some of the uses of the table are illustrated by the following four examples.

Example 1 — Equal Payments

Suppose the objective is to determine the present value of an income of $20,000 per year for fifteen years at 6 percent interest. Table 12 shows that the present value of $1,000 per year for fifteen years at 6 percent interest is $10,295. The present value of $20,000 per year would be 20 times that figure, or $205,900. In other words, the present value of the desired yearly income is determined by multiplying the appropriate figure from Table 12 by the number of thousands of dollars of desired yearly income.

Example 2 — Decreasing Payments

Suppose the objective is to determine the present value of an income of $20,000 per year for fifteen years, followed by an income of $12,000 per year for the subsequent twenty-five years, at 6 percent interest. The over-all income pattern may be viewed as $12,000 per year for the entire forty years, plus an additional $8,000 per year for the first fifteen years. The present value of $12,000 per year for forty years at 6 percent interest is $191,388 ($15,949 multiplied by 12). The present value of $8,000 per year for fifteen years at 6 percent interest is $82,360 ($10,295 multiplied by 8). The sum of these two results is $273,748 ($191,388 plus $82,360), which is the present

Table 12
Present Value of $1,000 per Year at Various Interest Rates
(payable at beginning of each year)

Number of Years	Interest Rates						
	0%	2%	4%	6%	8%	10%	12%
1	$ 1,000	$ 1,000	$ 1,000	$ 1,000	$ 1,000	$ 1,000	$ 1,000
2	2,000	1,980	1,962	1,943	1,926	1,909	1,893
3	3,000	2,942	2,886	2,833	2,783	2,736	2,690
4	4,000	3,884	3,775	3,673	3,577	3,487	3,402
5	5,000	4,808	4,630	4,465	4,312	4,170	4,037
6	6,000	5,713	5,452	5,212	4,993	4,791	4,605
7	7,000	6,601	6,242	5,917	5,623	5,355	5,111
8	8,000	7,742	7,002	6,582	6,206	5,868	5,564
9	9,000	8,325	7,733	7,210	6,747	6,335	5,968
10	10,000	9,162	8,435	7,802	7,247	6,759	6,328
11	11,000	9,983	9,111	8,360	7,710	7,145	6,650
12	12,000	10,787	9,760	8,887	8,139	7,495	6,938
13	13,000	11,575	10,385	9,384	8,536	7,814	7,194
14	14,000	12,348	10,986	9,853	8,904	8,103	7,424
15	15,000	13,106	11,563	10,295	9,244	8,367	7,628
16	16,000	13,849	12,118	10,712	9,559	8,606	7,811
17	17,000	14,578	12,652	11,106	9,851	8,823	7,974
18	18,000	15,292	13,166	11,477	10,122	9,022	8,120
19	19,000	15,992	13,659	11,828	10,372	9,201	8,250
20	20,000	16,678	14,134	12,158	10,604	9,365	8,366
25	25,000	19,914	16,247	13,550	11,529	9,985	8,784
30	30,000	22,844	17,984	14,591	12,158	10,370	9,022
35	35,000	25,499	19,411	15,368	12,587	10,609	9,157
40	40,000	27,903	20,584	15,949	12,879	10,757	9,233
45	45,000	30,080	21,549	16,383	13,077	10,849	9,276
50	50,000	32,052	22,341	16,708	13,212	10,906	9,301
55	55,000	33,838	22,993	16,950	13,304	10,942	9,315
60	60,000	35,456	23,528	17,131	13,367	10,964	9,323
65	65,000	36,921	23,969	17,266	13,409	10,978	9,327
70	70,000	38,249	24,330	17,368	13,438	10,986	9,330

value of an income of $20,000 per year for fifteen years, followed by an income of $12,000 per year for the subsequent twenty-five years, at 6 percent interest.

Example 3 — Increasing Payments

Suppose the objective is to determine the present value of an income of $12,000 per year for fifteen years, followed by an income of $20,000 per year for the subsequent twenty-five years, at 6 percent interest. The over-all income pattern may be viewed as $20,000 per year for the entire forty years, *minus* $8,000 per year for the first fifteen years. The present value of $20,000 per year for forty years at 6 percent interest is $318,980 ($15,949 multiplied by 20). The present value of $8,000 per year for fifteen years at 6 percent interest is $82,360 ($10,295 multiplied by 8). The difference between these two results is $236,620 ($318,980 minus $82,360), which is the present value of an income of $12,000 per year for fifteen years, followed by an income of $20,000 per year for the subsequent twenty-five years, at 6 percent interest.

Example 4 — Delayed Equal Payments

Suppose the objective is to determine the present value of an income of $20,000 per year for twenty-five years, with the income to start fifteen years from now, at 6 percent interest. The over-all income pattern may be viewed as $20,000 per year for the entire forty years, *minus* $20,000 per year for the first fifteen years. The present value of $20,000 per year for forty years at 6 percent interest is $318,980 ($15,949 multiplied by 20). The present value of $20,000 per year for fifteen years at 6 percent interest is $205,900 ($10,295 multiplied by 20). The difference between these two results is $113,080 ($318,980 minus $205,900), which is the present value of an income of $20,000 per year for twenty-five years, with the income to start fifteen years from now, at 6 percent interest.

Appendix B
Companies with Ten Consecutive Years of Top
Ratings in the 1975–1984 Life-Health Editions of
Best's Insurance Reports

Full Name of Company	Home Office Location
Acacia Mutual Life Insurance Company	Washington, DC
Aetna Life Insurance Company	Hartford, CT
Aid Association for Lutherans	Appleton, WI
Allstate Life Insurance Company	Northbrook, IL
American General Life Insurance Company	Houston, TX
American Mutual Life Insurance Company	Des Moines, IA
American National Insurance Company	Galveston, TX
American United Life Insurance Company	Indianapolis, IN
Bankers Life Company	Des Moines, IA
Banner Life Insurance Company (DC)	Rockville, MD
California–Western States Life Insurance Company	Sacramento, CA
The Canada Life Assurance Company	Toronto, Canada
Central Life Assurance Company	Des Moines, IA
Commonwealth Life Insurance Company	Louisville, KY
Confederation Life Insurance Company	Toronto, Canada
Connecticut General Life Insurance Company	Hartford, CT
Connecticut Mutual Life Insurance Company	Hartford, CT
Continental American Life Insurance Company	Wilmington, DE
Country Life Insurance Company	Bloomington, IL
Crown Life Insurance Company	Toronto, Canada
The Dominion Life Assurance Company	Waterloo, Canada
Durham Life Insurance Company	Raleigh, NC
The Equitable Life Assurance Society of the United States	New York, NY
Equitable Life Insurance Company	McLean, VA
Equitable Life Insurance Company of Iowa	Des Moines, IA
Farm Bureau Life Insurance Company	West Des Moines, IA
The Franklin Life Insurance Company	Springfield, IL
General American Life Insurance Company	St. Louis, MO
Great Southern Life Insurance Company	Houston, TX
The Great-West Life Assurance Company	Winnipeg, Canada
Guarantee Mutual Life Company	Omaha, NE
The Guardian Life Insurance Company of America	New York, NY

Appendix B — Continued

Full Name of Company	Home Office Location
Hartford Life Insurance Company	Hartford, CT
Home Beneficial Life Insurance Company	Richmond, VA
Home Life Insurance Company	New York, NY
IDS Life Insurance Company	Minneapolis, MN
The Imperial Life Assurance Company of Canada	Toronto, Canada
Indianapolis Life Insurance Company	Indianapolis, IN
Jefferson Standard Life Insurance Company	Greensboro, NC
John Hancock Mutual Life Insurance Company	Boston, MA
Kansas City Life Insurance Company	Kansas City, MO
Kansas Farm Life Insurance Company, Inc.	Manhattan, KS
Knights of Columbus	New Haven, CT
The Lafayette Life Insurance Company	Lafayette, IN
Lamar Life Insurance Company	Jackson, MS
Liberty Life Insurance Company	Greenville, SC
Liberty National Life Insurance Company	Birmingham, AL
Life and Casualty Insurance Company of Tennessee	Nashville, TN
Life Insurance Company of Georgia	Atlanta, GA
The Life Insurance Company of Virginia	Richmond, VA
The Lincoln National Life Insurance Company	Fort Wayne, IN
Lutheran Brotherhood	Minneapolis, MN
Lutheran Mutual Life Insurance Company	Waverly, IA
The Manufacturers Life Insurance Company	Toronto, Canada
Massachusetts Mutual Life Insurance Company	Springfield, MA
Metropolitan Life Insurance Company	New York, NY
The Midland Mutual Life Insurance Company	Columbus, OH
Midwestern United Life Insurance Company	Fort Wayne, IN
The Minnesota Mutual Life Insurance Company	St. Paul, MN
Monarch Life Insurance Company	Springfield, MA
Monumental Life Insurance Company	Baltimore, MD
Mutual Benefit Life Insurance Company	Newark, NJ
The Mutual Life Insurance Company of New York	New York, NY
Mutual Trust Life Insurance Company	Oak Brook, IL
National Fidelity Life Insurance Company (MO)	Overland Park, KS
National Guardian Life Insurance Company	Madison, WI
The National Life & Accident Insurance Company	Nashville, TN
National Life Insurance Company	Montpelier, VT

Appendix B — Continued

Full Name of Company	Home Office Location
National Travelers Life Company	Des Moines, IA
Nationwide Life Insurance Company	Columbus, OH
New England Mutual Life Insurance Company	Boston, MA
New York Life Insurance Company	New York, NY
North American Company for Life and Health Insurance	Chicago, IL
North American Life Assurance Company	Toronto, Canada
North American Reassurance Company	New York, NY
Northern Life Insurance Company	Seattle, WA
The Northwestern Mutual Life Insurance Company	Milwaukee, WI
Northwestern National Life Insurance Company	Minneapolis, MN
The Ohio National Life Insurance Company	Cincinnati, OH
Ohio State Life Insurance Company	Columbus, OH
Pacific Mutual Life Insurance Company	Newport Beach, CA
Pan-American Life Insurance Company	New Orleans, LA
The Paul Revere Life Insurance Company	Worcester, MA
The Penn Mutual Life Insurance Company	Philadelphia, PA
Peoples Life Insurance Company, Washington, DC (DC)	Durham, NC
Phoenix Mutual Life Insurance Company	Hartford, CT
Pilot Life Insurance Company	Greensboro, NC
Presbyterian Ministers' Fund	Philadelphia, PA
Provident Mutual Life Insurance Company of Philadelphia	Philadelphia, PA
The Prudential Insurance Company of America	Newark, NJ
Security Mutual Life Insurance Company of New York	Binghamton, NY
Shenandoah Life Insurance Company	Roanoke, VA
Southern Farm Bureau Life Insurance Company	Jackson, MS
Southwestern Life Insurance Company	Dallas, TX
Standard Insurance Company	Portland, OR
State Farm Life and Accident Assurance Company	Bloomington, IL
State Farm Life Insurance Company	Bloomington, IL
Sun Life Assurance Company of Canada	Toronto, Canada
Sun Life Insurance Company of America	Baltimore, MD
Sunset Life Insurance Company of America	Olympia, WA
Teachers Insurance and Annuity Association of America	New York, NY

Appendix B—Continued

Full Name of Company	Home Office Location
Transamerica Occidental Life Insurance Company	Los Angeles, CA
The Union Central Life Insurance Company	Cincinnati, OH
Union National Life Insurance Company	Baton Rouge, LA
United American Insurance Company (DE)	Dallas, TX
United Farm Bureau Family Life Insurance Company	Indianapolis, IN
United of Omaha Life Insurance Company	Omaha, NE
United Services Life Insurance Company	Washington, DC
The United States Life Insurance Company in the City of New York	New York, NY
USAA Life Insurance Company	San Antonio, TX
The Volunteer State Life Insurance Company	Chattanooga, TN
Washington National Insurance Company	Evanston, IL
The Western and Southern Life Insurance Company	Cincinnati, OH
Wisconsin National Life Insurance Company	Oshkosh, WI
Woodmen of the World Life Insurance Society and/or Omaha Woodmen Life Insurance Society	Omaha, NE

Appendix C
Addresses of State Insurance Regulatory Officials

Alabama:
Commissioner of Insurance
135 South Union Street
Montgomery, AL 36130

Alaska:
Director of Insurance
Pouch "D"
Juneau, AK 99811

American Samoa:
Insurance Commissioner
Office of the Governor
Pago Pago, AS 96797

Arizona:
Director of Insurance
1601 West Jefferson
Phoenix, AZ 85007

Arkansas:
Insurance Commissioner
400 University Tower Building
12th and University Streets
Little Rock, AR 72204

California:
Insurance Commissioner
600 South Commonwealth
14th Floor
Los Angeles, CA 90005

Colorado:
Commissioner of Insurance
303 West Colfax Avenue
5th Floor
Denver, CO 80204

Connecticut:
Insurance Commissioner
165 Capitol Avenue
State Office Building
Hartford, CT 06106

Delaware:
Insurance Commissioner
21 The Green
Dover, DE 19901

District of Columbia:
Superintendent of Insurance
614 "H" Street, N.W.
Suite 512
Washington, DC 20001

Florida:
Insurance Commissioner
State Capitol
Plaza Level Eleven
Tallahassee, FL 32301

Georgia:
Insurance Commissioner
200 Piedmont Avenue, S.E.
West Tower—7th Floor
Atlanta, GA 30334

Guam:
Insurance Commissioner
P. O. Box 2796
Agana, GU 96910

Hawaii:
Insurance Commissioner
P. O. Box 3614
Honolulu, HI 96811

Idaho:
Director of Insurance
700 West State Street
Boise, ID 83720

Illinois:
Director of Insurance
320 West Washington Street
4th Floor
Springfield, IL 62767

Appendix C—Continued

Indiana:
Commissioner of Insurance
509 State Office Building
Indianapolis, IN 46204

Iowa:
Commissioner of Insurance
State Office Building, G23
Ground Floor
Des Moines, IA 50319

Kansas:
Commissioner of Insurance
420 S.W. 9th Street
Topeka, KS 66612

Kentucky:
Insurance Commissioner
151 Elkhorn Court
Frankfort, KY 40601

Louisiana:
Commissioner of Insurance
950 North 5th Street
P. O. Box 44214
Baton Rouge, LA 70804

Maine:
Superintendent of Insurance
State Office Building
State House, Station 34
Augusta, ME 04333

Maryland:
Insurance Commissioner
501 St. Paul Place
7th Floor–South
Baltimore, MD 21202

Massachusetts:
Commissioner of Insurance
100 Cambridge Street
Boston, MA 02202

Michigan:
Insurance Commissioner
611 West Ottawa Street
P. O. Box 30220
Lansing, MI 48933

Minnesota:
Commissioner of Insurance
500 Metro Square Building
5th Floor
St. Paul, MN 55101

Mississippi:
Commissioner of Insurance
1804 Walter Sillers Building
P. O. Box 79
Jackson, MS 39205

Missouri:
Director of Insurance
301 West High Street 6 North
P. O. Box 690
Jefferson City, MO 65102

Montana:
Commissioner of Insurance
Mitchell Building
P. O. Box 4009
Helena, MT 59601

Nebraska:
Director of Insurance
301 Centennial Mall South
P. O. Box 94699
Lincoln, NE 68509

Nevada:
Commissioner of Insurance
Nye Building
201 South Fall Street
Carson City, NV 89710

Appendix C—Continued

New Hampshire:
Insurance Commissioner
169 Manchester Street
P. O. Box 2005
Concord, NH 03301

New Jersey:
Commissioner of Insurance
201 East State Street
Trenton, NJ 08625

New Mexico:
Superintendent of Insurance
PERA Building
P. O. Drawer 1269
Sante Fe, NM 87501

New York:
Superintendent of Insurance
160 West Broadway
New York, NY 10013

North Carolina:
Commissioner of Insurance
Dobbs Building
P. O. Box 26387
Raleigh, NC 27611

North Dakota:
Commissioner of Insurance
Capitol Building
Fifth Floor
Bismarck, ND 58505

Ohio:
Director of Insurance
2100 Stella Court
Columbus, OH 43215

Oklahoma:
Insurance Commissioner
408 Will Rogers Memorial Building
Oklahoma City, OK 73105

Oregon:
Insurance Commissioner
158–12th Street, N.E.
Salem, OR 97310

Pennsylvania:
Insurance Commissioner
Strawberry Square
13th Floor
Harrisburg, PA 17120

Puerto Rico:
Commissioner of Insurance
Fernandez Juncos Station
P. O. Box 8330
Santurce, PR 00910

Rhode Island:
Insurance Commissioner
100 North Main Street
Providence, RI 02903

South Carolina:
Chief Insurance Commissioner
2711 Middleburg Drive
P. O. Box 4067
Columbia, SC 29204

South Dakota:
Director of Insurance
Insurance Building
Pierre, SD 57501

Tennessee:
Commissioner of Insurance
114 State Office Building
Nashville, TN 37219

Texas:
Commissioner of Insurance
1110 San Jacinto Boulevard
Austin, TX 78786

Appendix C—Continued

Utah:
Commissioner of Insurance
160 East 300 South
P. O. Box 5803
Salt Lake City, UT 84110

Vermont:
Commissioner of Insurance
State Office Building
Montpelier, VT 05602

Virginia:
Commissioner of Insurance
700 Jefferson Building
P. O. Box 1157
Richmond, VA 23209

Virgin Islands:
Commissioner of Insurance
P. O. Box 450
Charlotte Amalie
St. Thomas, VI 00801

Washington:
Insurance Commissioner
Insurance Building AQ 21
Olympia, WA 98504

West Virginia:
Insurance Commissioner
2100 Washington Street, E.
Charleston, WV 25305

Wisconsin:
Commissioner of Insurance
123 West Washington Avenue
P. O. Box 7873
Madison, WI 53707

Wyoming:
Insurance Commissioner
2424 Pioneer Avenue
Cheyenne, WY 82002

Appendix D
Formula for Yearly Prices

The purpose of this appendix is to explain the formula for calculating the yearly price per $1,000 of protection, assuming a rate of return on the savings component. The formula is as follows:

$$YPT = \frac{(P + CVP)(1 + i) - (CV + D)}{(DB - CV)(.001)}$$

where

YPT = yearly price per $1,000 of protection
P = annual premium
CVP = cash value at end of preceding year
i = assumed rate of return on savings component, expressed as a decimal
CV = cash value at end of year
D = annual dividend
DB = death benefit

Explanation of the Formula

Consider the numerator of the formula. The first parenthetical expression $(P + CVP)$ is the amount you would have available to put into some other savings medium if you surrender the policy at the end of the preceding year. You would receive the cash value (CVP), and you would be relieved of the annual premium (P).

Multiplying the above expression by $(1 + i)$ tells you what you would have in the other savings medium by the end of the year if you invested the $(P + CVP)$ at an annual interest rate of i.

The last parenthetical expression in the numerator of the formula $(CV + D)$ is the amount you would have available at the end of the year if you continue the policy. The difference between the product of the first two expressions in the numerator and the last expression in the numerator is the yearly price of the life insurance protection.

Now consider the denominator of the formula. The cash value is the savings component of the policy, and you should view it as an asset. The life insurance protection you had, therefore, is the difference between the death benefit (DB) and the cash value (CV). The other expression in the denominator (.001) moves the decimal point three places to the left, so the denominator represents the yearly amount of life insurance protection in thousands of dollars.

Appendix D—Continued

Since the numerator is the yearly price you paid for the protection (assuming an interest rate of i), and since the denominator is the yearly amount of protection in thousands of dollars, the quotient is the yearly price per $1,000 of protection (assuming an interest rate of i).

The Assumed Interest Rate

The interest rate you assume is not important if the policy has little or no cash value. The interest rate you assume is important, however, if the policy has a substantial cash value.

You should select an interest rate based on what you believe you could earn in another savings medium with comparable safety and liquidity. Bear in mind, however, that the savings medium you are considering may produce interest income that is subject to current income taxation. The interest earnings built into cash-value life insurance, on the other hand, are income-tax-deferred and eventually will be either partially or fully income-tax-exempt.

Furthermore, you should not select an interest rate higher than the policy loan interest rate. If you believe you can earn a higher interest rate in another savings medium with comparable safety and liquidity, you should consider borrowing against the policy and investing the money in that alternate savings medium.

At various points in this book, the suggestion is made that you assume an interest rate of 6 percent. At other points, the suggestion is made that you assume an interest rate equal to the gross interest rate used by the company (in the case of universal life) or a hypothetical gross annual rate of investment return (in the case of variable life).

Appendix E
Formula for Yearly Rates of Return

The purpose of this appendix is to explain the formula for calculating the yearly rate of return on the savings component, assuming a price for the protection component. The formula is as follows:

$$i = \frac{(CV + D) + (YPT)(DB - CV)(.001)}{(P + CVP)} - 1$$

where

i = yearly rate of return on savings component, expressed as a decimal

CV = cash value at end of year

D = annual dividend

YPT = assumed yearly price per $1,000 of protection

DB = death benefit

P = annual premium

CVP = cash value at end of preceding year

Explanation of the Formula

The formula is the same as the formula in Appendix D, except that the terms have been rearranged so that i is left of the equal sign and YPT is right of the equal sign. In this sense, the formula for yearly rates of return is a mirror image of the formula for yearly prices per $1,000 of protection.

The formula for yearly rates of return may be explained in another way, however. The first expression in the numerator of the formula is the amount available in the policy at the end of the year. The second expression in the numerator is the assumed price of the protection component, which is determined by multiplying the amount of protection by an assumed price per $1,000 of protection. The denominator of the formula is the amount available in the policy at the beginning of the year.

As in any savings medium where nothing is deposited or withdrawn during the year, when the amount in the account at the end of the year is divided by the amount in the account at the beginning of the year, the quotient, minus one, is the yearly rate of return on the account expressed as a decimal.

The Assumed Yearly Price

You should select a yearly price based on what you believe the protection is worth to you. One way to do this is to survey the prices of one-year renewable term insurance in the market.

Appendix E—Continued

In this book, the suggestion is made that you assume certain benchmark prices. These were derived from certain United States population death rates. The benchmark figure for each five-year age bracket is close to the death rate per 1,000 at the highest age in that bracket. In other words, the benchmarks are close to the "raw material cost" of life insurance—that is, close to the amount needed to pay death claims based on population death rates.

Note that you should not calculate a yearly price per $1,000 of protection with the formula in Appendix D and then use that figure as the assumed yearly price in the formula here. If you do, you will come right back to the assumed rate of return used in the price formula. For example, suppose you assume 6 percent in the price formula, calculate a yearly price per $1,000 of protection, and then use the result as the assumed yearly price per $1,000 of protection in the formula here. In that case, your yearly rate of return would be 6 percent, and you would have engaged in a meaningless exercise.

Index

The Author

Joseph M. Belth is professor of insurance in the School of Business at Indiana University (Bloomington). He is also editor of *The Insurance Forum*, a four-page monthly periodical. For one of his books, *Participating Life Insurance Sold by Stock Companies*, he received the 1966 Elizur Wright Award for "outstanding original contribution to the literature of insurance." He has also received six awards for articles published in the *Journal of Risk and Insurance*.

Belth holds an AAS degree from Auburn (NY) Community College (now Cayuga County Community College), a BS degree *summa cum laude* from Syracuse University, and a PhD degree from the University of Pennsylvania. He also holds the CLU (Chartered Life Underwriter) and CPCU (Chartered Property and Casualty Underwriter) designations.

Belth was a life insurance agent in Syracuse for five years before beginning his graduate study. Following completion of his graduate study, he served for one year on the staff of the American Society of CLU and The American College. He has been a member of the Indiana University faculty since 1962, and served for five years as chairman of the university's committee on insurance and retirement systems. He served for nine years on the editorial staff of the *Journal of Risk and Insurance*.

Belth is a past president of the American Risk and Insurance Association, an organization of insurance professors and others interested in insurance education. He was the subject of a page-one profile in the January 5, 1978 issue of *The Wall Street Journal*, and was also profiled in the June 8, 1981 issue of *Barron's*.